CRAFT AND SPIRIT

Psychoanalytic Inquiry Book Series

Volume 20

Psychoanalytic Inquiry Book Series

Vol. 1: *Reflections on Self Psychology*—Joseph D. Lichtenberg & Samuel Kaplan (eds.)

Vol. 2: *Psychoanalysis and Infant Research*—Joseph D. Lichtenberg

Vol. 4: *Structures of Subjectivity: Explorations in Psychoanalytic Phenomenology*—George E. Atwood & Robert D. Stolorow

Vol. 7: *The Borderline Patient: Emerging Concepts in Diagnosis, Psychodynamics, and Treatment, Vol. 2*—James S. Grotstein, Marion F. Solomon & Joan A. Lang (eds.)

Vol. 8: *Psychoanalytic Treatment: An Intersubjective Approach*—Robert D. Stolorow, Bernard Brandchaft & George E. Atwood

Vol. 9: *Female Homosexuality: Choice without Volition*—Elaine V. Siegel

Vol. 10: *Psychoanalysis and Motivation*—Joseph D. Lichtenberg

Vol. 11: *Cancer Stories: Creativity and Self-Repair*—Esther Dreifuss Kattan

Vol. 12: *Contexts of Being: The Intersubjective Foundations of Psychological Life*—Robert D. Stolorow & George E. Atwood

Vol. 13: *Self and Motivational Systems: Toward a Theory of Psychoanalytic Technique*—Joseph D. Lichtenberg, Frank M. Lachmann & James L. Fosshage

Vol. 14: *Affects as Process: An Inquiry into the Centrality of Affect in Psychological Life*—Joseph M. Jones

Vol. 15: *Understanding Therapeutic Action: Psychodynamic Concepts of Cure*—Lawrence E. Lifson (ed.)

Vol. 16: *The Clinical Exchange: Techniques Derived from Self and Motivational Systems*—Joseph D. Lichtenberg, Frank M. Lachmann & James L. Fosshage

Vol. 17: *Working Intersubjectively: Contextualism in Psychoanalytic Practice*—Donna M. Orange, George E. Atwood & Robert D. Stolorow

Vol. 18: *Kohut, Loewald, and the Postmoderns: A Comparative Study of Self and Relationship*—Judith Guss Teicholz

Vol. 19: *A Spirit of Inquiry: Communication in Psychoanalysis*—Joseph D. Lichtenberg, Frank M. Lachmann & James L. Fosshage

Vol. 20: *Craft and Spirit: A Guide to the Exploratory Psychotherapies*—Joseph D. Lichtenberg

Craft and Spirit

A Guide to the Exploratory Psychotherapies

Joseph D. Lichtenberg

THE ANALYTIC PRESS
2005 Hillsdale, NJ London

Published by
The Analytic Press, Inc., Publishers
Editorial Offices:
101 West Street
Hillsdale, NJ 07642

www.analyticpress.com

Library of Congress Cataloging-in-Publication Data

Lichtenberg, Joseph D.
Craft and spirit : a guide to the exploratory psychotherapies /
Joseph D. Lichtenberg.
p. cm. — (Psychoanalytic inquiry book series ; v. 20)
Includes bibliographical references and index.
ISBN 0-88163-433-6
1. Psychoanalysis. 2. Psychotherapy. I. Title. II. Series.

RC504.L525 2005
616.89'14-dc22

2005043645

Printed in the United States of America

10 9 8 7 6 5 4 3 2 1

CONTENTS

INTRODUCTION

WHAT JUSTIFIES YET ANOTHER BOOK ABOUT techniques for the intensive psychotherapies? And why now? Twenty-five years ago, I wrote *"The Talking Cure": A Descriptive Guide to Psychoanalysis.* That book, like this one, was written to inform not only patients contemplating intensive psychotherapy but also experienced therapists and those in training. My approach was to combine classical analytic theory and technique with new contributions being made by self psychology. What contemporary changes call for a new presentation, a presentation that shifts from analysis as a separate entity, to an inclusive view of exploratory psychotherapies?

Within the field, we have come to an understanding that no rigid boundary separates psychoanalysis from other intensive, investigative psychotherapies. The guidelines for technique I present here are equally applicable to analysis and all other exploratory psychotherapies. The biggest difference between analysis and psychotherapy lies not in the principles of technique used, but in the opportunity provided by the frequency of the sessions and an open-ended mutual commitment. This book is addressed to patients considering intensive psychotherapy or analysis, or who are deciding between them.

Similarly, the technique guidelines I propose are directed to therapists practicing psychotherapy, psychoanalysis, or both.

Over the quarter century since "*The Talking Cure*," I have become increasingly convinced that, to a greater extent than had been thought previously, therapists must sense themselves, and be sensed by their patients, as fully and emotionally involved in the treatment. The value once attributed to silence, abstinence, neutrality, and anonymity has been tested and found wanting. The duality of patient–therapist cannot be characterized by the subjectivity of the patient and a presumed objectivity of the therapist, but by two interactive subjectivities. Therapists and analysts must be willing and able, by virtue of their training, to place themselves on stage with their patients to explore the drama that unfolds from the patient's experience and problems. Life is lived with people, and therapy cannot be otherwise. A reconsideration of the restrictive approach that followed Freud's papers on technique and informed ego psychology was called for by theorists as diverse as Sullivan, Winnicott, Stone, Bowlby, Rogers, Klein, Greenson, Loewald, Tomkins, Stolorow, and Kohut. Advocating, however, that therapists be more involved, more participant, more on stage, introduces hazards long recognized and feared: intrusiveness, encouraging undesirable dependence, and, worst of all, interfering with the openness to explore that constitutes an investigative psychotherapy. In this book, I present guidelines for technique that are designed to permit and encourage therapists in their greater involvement and transparency while not only preserving but greatly enhancing exploration.

The theoretical foundation for the principles of technique I advocate derives from research on infants and young children. This broadly based research contributes many salient conceptions relevant to my proposals and descriptions. Regulation of emotion, action, and motivation is dyadic (caregiver and infant), intrafamily (father–mother–child), and via peer-group interactional learning. Communication begins between a verbal caregiver and a nonverbal, presymbolic infant. Subsequently, communicative messages are conveyed both in nonverbal gestures and interactions and in syntactic or metaphoric verbalizations. Stated more simply, dyads, such as therapists and patients, communicate by both spoken and nonverbal interactions. Therefore, in the dyadic realm of an exploratory treatment, two parallel tracks of communication are unfolding: a verbal exchange and an enactive pull to involve one another in roles expressive of the motives and experiences of each participant. Because all communication involves various degrees of verbalization and enactment, no longer can we ask whether therapists should be involved as participants; rather, we must ask how they cannot. A contemporary view of therapy requires guidelines for technique that position therapists optimally to comprehend both verbal and enactive messages.

Another reason for a fresh consideration of exploratory guidelines arises from a changed perspective on the problems patients bring. In the past, many analysts believed that only those patients with specific psychoneurotic symptoms were suitable for psychoanalysis. Psychoneurotic patients were assumed to be fully able to free associate and bring to conscious awareness unconscious conflicts and complexes as soon as repression, isolation, projection, and other mechanisms of defense were recognized and interpreted. Such ideal-for-analysis patients have proven to be extremely rare, and analysts have become increasingly sensitive to personality and characterological problems and to the many impediments that limit free association. Stated in today's language, most patients bring to therapy backgrounds of insecure attachment and serious concerns about safety and being again traumatized. Their associative flow reflects constraints evidenced by speech that is either preoccupied and self-absorbed, or dismissive and avoidant. Indeed, some closer-to-the-ideal patients who have had basically secure attachments do come for exploratory therapy. They are able to experience greater safety and fewer constraints on their communication, especially verbal communication. The majority of patients, however, are those for whom classical psychoanalysis had been considered unsuitable, but now we are able fully to approach these patients through exploratory guidelines such as those I describe in this volume. Although verbal communication remains no less important, we can treat a more extensive and diverse group of patients through recognition of the many affect states and altered cognitions that characterize nonverbal communication and contribute to enactments.

In this book, I refer frequently to how therapists focus their attention. Originally, a therapist's ideal focus was regarded to be that of an objective observer identifying the contents (fantasies, conflicts, complexes) of the patient's psyche. To protect the hoped for objectivity of their observations, therapists scrutinized themselves for any interference to their neutral listening and interpreting that might arise from conflicts of their own that were activated by the patient's unfolding motivations. Therapists' observations of the inner worlds of patients and their own remain fully significant. Therapists no longer aim to achieve or protect objectivity; rather, they attempt to tune in as closely as possible to the subjectivities of the two participants in the therapeutic dyad. Focusing on subjectivity shifts the emphasis from an outside observer to an empathic attempt to sense patients' inner worlds from within their perspectives. Focusing on subjectivity also shifts the emphasis away from therapists' scrutinizing their inner worlds to prevent loss of objectivity and toward regarding their associations and emotions as sources of data critical for exploration. In the course of the exploratory effort, another focus is created. From the communication they share, therapist and patient create a dynamic process of what is transpiring *between* them, an *intersubjective* realm that emerges from their collaborative experience. Thus, we must focus attention on the unique subjectivities of the two individuals and the unique, intersubjective, dynamic, communicative flow they create. A therapist's empathic listening helps to explore the patient's subjectivity and motivations; the therapist's introspection opens her subjectivity and motivations to herself; and the therapist's attention to the affective interplay between them opens their intersubjectivity for exploration. The latter is critical for an inquiry into enactments. Stated simply, contemporary technique expands the questions we ask. A therapist still asks, what do your associations, your dreams, the verbal and imagistic symbolic expressions you communicate, tell me about your inner world? A therapist still asks, is some pull from some unresolved problem of mine interfering with my ability to be involved and attentive. A therapist is especially likely to ask, what does this belief about, or fantasy of, or this memory of our work together, tell me about what a patient is trying to express? And an added question, especially needed for the treatment of more troubled patients, is what is going on between us? How is it, and what does it mean, that the atmosphere has turned cold and stilted; antagonistic and oppositional; erotic with mutual joking and teasing; boring, repetitive, and flat; edgy and frightening?

Infant and developmental research provide another clarifying perspective that therapists can use to structure the boundaries of their interventions as they move into more "on stage" involvement. Many useful analogies have been drawn between caregiver–child and therapist–patient interactions: the centrality of emotional recognition; the establishing of a secure base through mirroring, affirming, and sharing of intimacy; and the development of mutual respect. Equally significant are being able to be with one another while still retaining one's own initiative and perspectives, and being able to be apart without feeling abandoned and isolated. All of these are factors in both caregiving and therapy, but the analogy should not be carried too far. The caregiver–child relationship is of necessity very tilted, whereas the moments of tilt in the therapist–patient experience must be combined with recognition of an essential adult-to-adult equality. The distinction becomes clearer when we consider the role of provision and inquiry in both child rearing and in exploratory therapies. Infant and parent must get to know the other and who one is to the other. The purpose of this ongoing inquiry is that the parent can thus better provide for the infant's needs, and the infant can thus better signal those needs. In child rearing, inquiry has the goal of facilitating provision. Alternatively, in the intensive psychotherapies, inquiry rather than provision, is fundamental. Of course provision plays a part; some degree of provision is necessary for an exploration to take place. Further, once an exploration is underway, for patients to feel that they are understood, that their motives and difficulties are recognized, becomes in itself a highly valued provision.

Yet how are the great variety of patients' needs, desires, goals, and values to be reckoned with? Provision is not a therapist's guiding principle in responding to a patient's needs and desires for physiological requirements, intimacy beyond the bounds of the treatment, revenge, escape, a marriage partner, directive guidance, sensual pleasure, erotic excitement, sparring, blaming, denunciation, and a multitude of other cravings of which humans are capable. To say that a response of provision lies outside the therapist's goal is too simplistic, however. The pulls on the therapist for more direct responses to many if not all of the patient's cravings (and the therapist's own) create a far from clear set of boundaries. Dealing with the powerful affects generated by human desire is, and has to be, "messy" at times. So what guides the clinical exchange to keep it from degenerating into a futile attempt at reparative parenting or from going so far with provision that it resembles adoption? I believe the answer lies in what I describe as "a spirit of inquiry." A spirit of inquiry is the therapist's gyroscope, helping to re-right the therapeutic endeavor when the immediacy of exploration is lost in the heat of struggles over a patient's pressure for provisionary responses. The ability of therapists to maintain a spirit of inquiry throughout a long, emotion-laden, clinical endeavor depends on the therapist's deep conviction of the efficacy of exploration, the theories that guide them, and the techniques they employ. Conviction of that depth requires therapists to have extensive training and a successful encounter with their own inner worlds of desire, fantasy, beliefs, goals, and values and with all the revenants of their past, significant relationships. They must appreciate retaining an open mind, the influence of context, the high probability of error, and the unpredictability of many human responses. The guidelines for technique this book describes are based on the premise that the therapist begins the treatment imbued with a spirit of inquiry and maintains it through ups and downs of confusion, alternating with understanding, and understanding alternating with bewildering enactments. Patients enter therapy with whatever goals of symptom relief or changes in personality or life situation that they wish to achieve—provision minded we might say. The guidelines I espouse are designed to help patients to feel safe enough, to remain patient enough, to become invested in exploring and thereby join the therapist in adopting a spirit of inquiry. Those moments when a spirit of inquiry becomes shared, despite whatever messy exchange fills the foreground of their interaction, are the moments when exploration in depth takes hold, and lasting change becomes increasingly possible.

I hope to impart to the reader a sense of the craft involved in the exploratory therapies. By craft I mean skill—not only the skill of therapists to be effective therapists, but also their skill in helping patients to be effective patients. By craft I also mean an activity that touches on artistry and creativity and moves "technique" away from rules and ritual. My guidelines are meant to help both participants develop this artistry. To be effective, however, guidelines for exploration must be based on solid principles of technique. In this book, I combine the ten principles of technique Lachmann, Fosshage, and I described previously with guidelines that make their procedural application clearer. I try to present the "craft" largely through many clinical examples that illustrate the guidelines in action.

A spirit of inquiry, I believe, imbues the craft with its liveliness of sustained purpose. The spirit of inquiry derives from the humanist tradition brought to psychoanalysis by Freud and sometimes lost in Freud's concern that he be taken seriously as a scientist. The humanist spirit shines brightly in the writings of all my heroes in the psychoanalytic tradition—Ferenczi, Kohut, Winnicott, Stone, Greenson, Bowlby, and Hill. A spirit of inquiry is thus the ineffable something more than the craft and the doing of listening, understanding, and interpreting. It is the humanist trend that combines a healer's altruism with a therapist's approach to exploration through sensing into another to gain a depth of knowledge of the other, the self, and the emergent experiential world they create together.

PLAN

The plan I follow is to present ten chapters. In each chapter I describe one of the ten guidelines for technique that had been presented in *The Clinical Exchange*. In *The Clinical Exchange*, we used a single case to illustrate the guidelines. Here, I give numerous examples to help the reader understand what is meant by each guideline. Some of the cases are based on previously published clinical examples, others are unpublished previously.

The guidelines originated from suggestions I have made to therapists I supervised in the past. I noticed that I was making similar recommendations repeatedly and decided to keep a record of them.

I discussed the recommendations with my colleagues and collaborators Frank Lachmann and James Fosshage. We agreed with their value, changed the wording for clarity, and arranged the order. We formulated our ideas further in *A Spirit of Inquiry*. Thus, although in this book, I speak with an authorial "I," what I present is a composite of our triad, as well as many suggestions and criticisms from others: my close friends and colleagues Alan Kindler, Ernest Wolf, Estelle Shane, Jay and Lynn Bisgyer, and Rosemary Segalla. Mary Main, Diana Diamond, and Sidney Blatt have helped me broaden my knowledge of attachment research. Melvin Bornstein, Lawrence Friedman, and Henry Smith have helped me broaden my knowledge in the entire field of psychoanalysis. Arthur Malin, Ronald Bodansky, Gianni Nebbiosi, William Coburn, Fred Hilkert, and Sandra Hershberg, my colleagues in self psychology, have been invariably supportive. Paul Stepansky has been much more than a supportive publisher; he has offered much useful conceptual advice. The contributions of my patients, as well as my supervisees and their patients, are truly the vital ingredient that I cannot acknowledge sufficiently.

I have made two choices about terminology. First, I have employed the designator "therapist" to include those who have graduated from analytic institutes and those who have received training in analytically oriented psychotherapy. I make this choice because the type of therapy I am describing is that of an intensive investigative approach, and the ten guidelines are designed for use across the full range of exploratory psychotherapies. The background I bring to my conceptualizing is primarily my experience as both a practicing psychoanalyst and psychotherapist. The second choice is to use either the plural for therapist and patient or to use "him" or "her" for either.

Chapter 1: A Facilitating Environment describes guidelines for beginning an exploratory therapy.

Chapter 2: Sensing into the Mind-States of Another presents guidelines to an exploring therapist's fundamental method of listening: the systematic application of the empathic mode of perception.

Chapter 3: Affects and the Pathway to Motivation; Chapter 4: "The Message Contains the Message"; and *Chapter 5: Filling the Narrative Envelope* provide more focused guidance to the therapist's listening, indicating priorities for hearing and understanding the message.

Chapter 6: "The Wearing of Attributions"; Chapter 7: Model Scenes: A Guide to Bringing the Theater of the Mind onto the Patient–Therapist Stage; and *Chapter 8: How to Respond to a Message that There Is Something a Patient Doesn't Want Himself, His Therapist, or Both to Know* guide therapists in the approach to transferences, enactments, and aversive manifestations.

Chapter 9: The Therapist Speaks discusses three ways in which therapists intervene to further the therapeutic process.

Chapter 10: Evaluating Progress describes following the sequence of interventions and patients' responses to them to evaluate their effect.

Coda integrates the guidelines with the principles of evaluation.

I recommend that readers hold two perspectives in mind as they consider the guidelines I propose for the exploratory psychotherapies. First, for therapists to effectively follow the guidelines, they must have developed considerable knowledge of and intimacy with themselves. They must have an awareness of their capacity for and difficulties with self-regulation under stress as well as the factors, present and past, of self-with-other influences that are shaping and have shaped their lived experiences. This degree of self-knowledge and introspective potential can only develop from their own participation as patients in an exploratory psychotherapy.

Second, the guidelines are based on a revised appreciation of the roles of past and present in effecting change. Traditionally, as indicated by Freud's archeological metaphor (see chapter 8), analysts used the present (symptoms, associations, behaviors, and dreams) to discover or uncover "truths" of the oedipal and preoedipal past. This theory presumed that the past that was creating disturbances in the present reflected distortions present in childhood conceptions of events. The distortions were regarded to be the inevitable outcome of untamed sexual and aggressive drives of infant, toddler, and young child. The uncovering of defensive layers therefore was necessary to reveal the distortions and correct them through an adult's knowledge of "reality."

My perspective reverses the traditional view that our goal is to use the present to discover the past. I hold that we use what we can surmise about the past to understand perplexing influences on here-and-now lived experience. My view is based on a theory of motivational systems that reflect self and mutual influences throughout life rather than a dual drive-distortion concept. From all here-and-now experiences, expectations form that influence the way individuals experience the next here and now. We can never fully understand the present of our patients or ourselves without an appreciation of the past. Our goal in exploratory therapies, however, is to open the present to understanding and change. Knowledge of the past is indispensable to that goal, but is not the goal in itself. Our focus on the present opens to us the possibility of empathic entry into a patient's emotions, thoughts, fantasies, and intentions—the fundamental guide to the approach I recommend.

Chapter 1

A FACILITATING ENVIRONMENT

WE (LICHTENBERG, LACHMANN, AND FOSSHAGE, 1996) have described the optimal environment as "arrangements that establish a frame of friendliness, consistency, reliability, and an ambiance of safety." Clinical experience has taught therapists much about the creation of an environment that facilitates an exploratory psychotherapy.

The boundaries and procedural aspects of therapy are spoken of as the "frame." Concretely, a frame is an enclosure and, in that sense, references an office and the physical surround, a commercial building, or rooms in a home. It is an environment a therapist selects for himself and his patients. The frame symbolizes other kinds of delineating and supportive arrangements, however, and in these less physical ways carries the imprint of patient as well as therapist. These include the timing of appointments, their duration, and the fee and payment arrangements. The critically important ambiance of safety develops from the collaborative creation of these arrangements. A mutual experience of safety evolves from creating a fit between the needs, desires, intentions, and goals of the treatment dyad. Like any delicate and subtle experience between two people, a sense of safety requires constant attention to the inevitable changes in fit between the needs, desires, and goals of patient and therapist as the therapy proceeds.

What is dyadic interaction? When does dyadic interaction begin? It begins in a patient's mind in his or her contemplation of entering treatment and forms around the name of the therapist and whatever information about him or her the patient has. Similarly for the therapist. Then the telephone contact, the answering machine message, the back and forth about setting the time of the first appointment, and sometimes a question about the fee. But the most telling beginning occurs on meeting in the waiting room.

The first face-to-face, eye-to-eye encounter is a poignant moment for both participants. Both bring with them their own experiences, motivations, and goals—some similar, some different. Some expectations, of which patient and therapist may or may not be aware, converge, making friendliness easier to create. Some expectations conflict, leading to a less comfortable beginning, ranging from an appropriately cautious feeling out of one another to open discomfort and mutual aversion.

THE MUTUAL CREATION OF THE FRAME

Before the therapist enters, the patient in the waiting room has already been primed toward an affective response. Rushing to get there, she might be breathless. Lost on the way, he might feel flustered. Entering a separate waiting room, she might feel pleased with the privacy. Entering a common waiting room, he might feel reluctant to be seen by others or relieved of shame to see others coming for treatment. Some patients are consciously sensitive to their surroundings: the modern or traditional furniture, soothing or stimulating wall colors, personally chosen art objects or impersonal functional choices, padded chairs to sink into or firm seats. Some patients do not respond overtly to the therapist's choices, but all take them in and sense either this is a good place, an OK place, or a doubtful place for them.

Greetings fulfill an important role in the repertoire of human exchanges. Beginning in the earliest moments and repeated many times daily with closely attached people, acquaintances, and strangers, greetings demonstrate a procedural memory, an implicit way of relating. A therapist, walking into the waiting room and greeting her patient with a friendly hello, I am Doctor, Ms., or Sally Brown, receives a tentative, but friendly response from a well-dressed business person. They shake hands, and they are easily poised for the task of getting acquainted. Their implicit nonverbal communication suggests a fair likelihood that they can form a secure attachment while they open channels into the problems that bring him to seek her professional help.

A therapist seeking to offer a friendly greeting but seeing the prospective patient looking like a "deer caught in the headlights" recognizes that he must shift his greeting to an acceptance of the frightened state of the person who is viewing the experience as an actual or potential trauma in itself. The therapist might move more slowly toward a fearful person and wait for a cue before making physical contact. A firm handshake from the patient might suggest that, although he was extremely anxious, he was substantially present emotionally. This reassurance would modify the therapist's need to respond immediately to the patient's anxiety.

Coming to meet Miss Janis, a biologist whose treatment had been interrupted by her transfer to Washington, I was startled to see her avoid all eye contact with me. For me, our contact began with an eerie feeling as she conducted herself in a businesslike fashion while conveying to me a sense that I was not there and that she had no recognition of the oddness of our interaction. Confronted with her avoidant-detached approach, I fell into the role of proceeding with the consultative interview, equally making no reference to its oddity. I was somewhat reassured as I noted that although she never made eye contact, she moved her head back and forth, taking in little glances at me, gradually expressing less affective flatness and detachment.

Mr. Drew, immediately on the heels of my greeting, launched into a description of the difficulty he had finding the office and his uncertainty about whether to come. As he walked from the waiting room to the office, he started to tell me about his wife. His responses to my opening questions were scattered, full of irrelevant detail, indicating easy distractibility and little opportunity for a good initial collaboration. He stopped himself momentarily, only to begin another story about his wife.

In their response to the moment of greeting, each of these patients revealed much about themselves, both explicitly in what they said and implicitly in how they communicated and interacted. Each of them provided a challenge for the therapist whose intention was to initiate a therapeutic experience. Therapists use different conceptual formulations to organize the experience and meaning of even such brief encounters as I have described. One way therapists attempt to meet this challenge is by formulating the patient's psychology or psychopathology. Traditionally, therapists have used diagnostic categories to identify patterns of illness. Thus, the terrified-looking patient might be thought of as having a panic disorder or a hysterical character. Miss Janis could be provisionally diagnosed as having a schizoid personality disorder, and Mr. Drew as being obsessional (obsessional–compulsive disorder). Diagnostic assessments provide therapists with a background of knowledge about psychological illnesses, prognoses, and possible treatment choices, particularly psychopharmicological. Such assessments are often necessary for insurance coverage. Diagnostic typologies, however, have the disadvantage of structuring the interaction as a tilted relationship between a labeling observer (therapist) examining an ill person (patient) with symptoms and personality disorders. Clinical experience has taught therapists that a tilted relationship is not consistent with the creation of safety, an essential component of the therapeutic relationship. A much better alternative to an emphasis on pathological formations is an adaptational perspective originally formulated by ego psychology and now reconceptualized by attachment research.

Attachment studies reveal that all infant–caretaker pairs develop a wide variety of interactional strategies for maintaining connectedness. From lived moments of early attachment experience, these strategies emerge to cope with perceived danger and loss. By one year of age, a securely attached child responds to a caregiver's return after a stressful absence via a strategy of distress, appeal, and positive response to comforting. Other infants express distress but are resistant to comfort, their insecurity demonstrated by their hesitance either to accept or move away from the caregiver. Other infants reveal no overt distress, although they have physiological signs indicative of stress. They appear indifferent to their mother's absence and avoid contact on her return. Their strategy seems to say that they can best maintain an emotional tie to the important other by keeping their distance from her and make no demands or other protests. Sadly, a significant number of one-year-olds (10%) have had such disrupted patterns or serious moments of caregiving lapses that they have been unable to form a consistent strategy to maintain a secure connection. They may shift from approach to withdrawal and from being overwhelmed by emotion to momentary states of detachment, disorientation, or dissociation.

Clearly on first meeting, or even after several consultative interviews, therapists must be extremely tentative in making either a diagnosis or identifying the patient's particular strategy for forming an attachment. Nonetheless, they are immediately confronted with the issue of creating a safe base for treatment. Unlike an observer attempting to be objective while making a diagnosis, a therapist beginning a therapeutic contact is necessarily a participant in the formation of an attachment. When working with a patient capable of establishing a secure attachment from which to explore the problems and vicissitudes of his life, most therapists will have little difficulty forming a therapeutic relationship. When confronted with a terrified patient, however, therapists will sense the existence of unresolved trauma and the requirement that they attempt to balance their desire for more information with the risk of triggering disorientation and further disorganization. Avoidant patients keep therapists at a distance while conveying the need to build bridges that permit contact despite the arid world that they cocreate. Preoccupied, chattering patients leave a trail of confusion and distress while filling the conversational space and shutting out the therapist whose orienting interventions are badly needed.

First meetings between a patient and a therapist are infused with a profound paradox. Two people meet who have made no commitment to each other and, as yet, have defined nothing of their individual and mutual plans. Yet from the beginning, they are, to a degree, already involved in what they are searching each other out to arrange. The patient is determined to find help in some explicit and implied manner, and the therapist is committed to providing it. Along with the paradox of patient and therapist already entering into the treatment that they have met to talk about beginning lies an additional complication of separate and competing self-interests that can easily interfere with therapeutic goals. Therapist and patient have to resolve divergent pulls involving money and convenience of time availability. Beyond the pragmatics of self-interest, however, lies a powerful, hard-to-define factor of how far each can stretch to meet the personal characteristics, the individuality of "being" that each conveys to the other. The impact of each on the other can be a dramatic love, or hate, or love–hate "on first sight" by either or both. More common are less dramatic factors of similarity or disparity of gender, age, appearance, culture, religion, interests, and especially style of communicating—that is, listening and talking.

Arrangements are worked out explicitly; that is, they are thought and spoken about in words. They are based on an assessment of the prospective patient's needs, the therapist's availability, and the meshing of time and payment requirements. Each person who is seeking treatment has a story to tell, one she means to tell, one she means to keep hidden until it is safe to tell, and one she is revealing inadvertently through gestures and modes of speech. Despite our altruistic intentions and humanitarian values, the therapy consultation has elements of the market place. The prospective patient is "selling" himself as a suitable person for treatment while convincing himself that he needs therapy and will benefit if he commits to it. The prospective therapist is "selling" herself to the patient to accept her as a trained competent practitioner of a professional discipline and to herself to believe that she can work therapeutically with this man and the challenges he presents. Further, the patient may be "auditioning" the prospective therapist, having several other appointments set up, while the therapist may be seeking a patient to fill a particular clinical or time spot or for a referral he wants to make to a colleague.

On the basis of this confusing array of multiple motives, I make every effort to clarify to the patient that we are engaged in a consultation the goal of which is to arrive at a recommendation. During the consultation, I will learn as much as I can about him in two or three meetings, and he will have an opportunity to sense what talking to and with me is like. I will give him an opportunity to ask me questions, and I will offer him my preliminary understanding of the problem and my recommendation. I assure him he will have time to consider and sleep on any decision we arrive at and encourage him to do so.

In arranging the frequency of sessions I tend to follow patterns used by many therapists. These patterns have changed in recent years. Traditionally, four or five times per week psychoanalysis was regarded as the optimal treatment of psychoneuroses and one or two times per week psychotherapy as better suited for more "troubled" conditions—borderline, mood, or addictive disorders. Because of changes in approach that I believe are more widespread as reflected in many contemporary psychoanalytic theories, analysts nowadays are less distant and silent. They are less concerned that their more active involvement will be construed as a gratification that will lessen a patient's motivation for treatment. As a consequence of their greater involvement (as I describe in later chapters), analyst/therapists have discovered that the treatment of more troubled patients is actually facilitated by the greater opportunity that more frequency permits. The benefits are twofold. First, the greater frequency offers more opportunities to recognize and discuss patterns (the same explicit benefit traditionally ascribed to the analysis of neurotic patients). Second, the consistency and reliability of the commitment offers a critical implicit benefit, a beneficial change that develops in the background, often outside of conscious awareness. The greater mutual opportunity and openness to explore facilitates growth in the implicit knowledge of how to work together effectively and in safety. Safety here does not mean freedom from disappointment, hurt, shame, and other kinds of disruption. This would be impossible for any therapist–patient pair regardless of the type of problem. Safety, in this context, means that, as much as possible, disruptions to the therapeutic relationship will be recognized, acknowledged, and explored. Alertness to disruptions, for therapist and patient, provides the optimal means to restore their mutual purpose, the ongoing pursuit of sustained inquiry and exploration.

When it comes to deciding on frequency of sessions, patterns of common usage may serve as guides, but each dyad is unique and involves the desires and constraints of the individuals involved. Some prospective patients regard greater frequency as a terrifying prospect. They may experience such a recommendation as indicating the therapist considers them to have severe psychopathology, thus evoking shame and dread. It may, for others, raise the specter of being too rapidly exposed or rendered dependent or vulnerable to exploitation. From my side as therapist/analyst, I recommend the frequency that I believe will give us the best start, given my appraisal of therapeutic needs and practical constraints. With the spirit of inquiry as my guide, the general approach I follow and the principles of technique I employ are essentially the same whether for one or five weekly sessions. Of course, the opportunity for continuity, for tracking communications, and for following up on themes and consolidating gains is greater with more frequent contact. I do not make this decision on the basis of traditional psychiatric diagnoses or the distinction between psychotherapy (one or two times per week) or psychoanalysis (three, four, or five per week). Rather, I try to arrive at a session frequency that will provide the optimal opportunity to help avoidant patients to feel safer revealing themselves, preoccupied patients to become more aware and organized, and patients with labile affect to experience more stability and calm.

By the end of the consultation, therapists have an impression of the session frequency to recommend and the acceptance or reluctant response their proposal is likely to trigger. I use a flexible approach. Although I recommend the treatment approach I believe to be optimal, I listen as open-mindedly as I can to the patient's response. If the patient accepts, does it indicate that, in our brief time together, we have already negotiated successfully? Or does the acceptance seem too quick, too much a submission to authority? If the patient objects, can we find common ground, or does the patient's request or demand indicate an insurmountable obstacle, calling for referral elsewhere? The search for a way to make an arrangement that will allow us to start in itself constitutes a beginning of treatment via the negotiation that takes place. Whatever plan we begin with, the ongoing negotiation of the ground rules for the frame arrangements continues through the treatment as a work in progress. By telling the patient my recommendation, even though I suspect the patient may not be prepared to accept that degree of commitment, I am opening the possibility of change as the treatment progresses. Of course, change can take place in either direction.

Fee arrangements can range from being simple and straightforward or complex and difficult. In any community, a "standard" fee for therapy sessions becomes established with variations. Graduates of psychoanalytic institutes often charge more than therapists without analytic training. Psychiatrists (MDs) often set fees higher than psychologists (PhDs), whose fees are apt to be higher than social workers (LCSWs). More experienced and better-known analysts and therapists may set higher charges, but often not. Almost all analysts and therapists have some variation or sliding scale, from "usual" to highest and lowest acceptable, and the scales of therapists and analysts in training may slide the lowest. Many communities have clinics that offer competent, unsupervised and supervised, therapy at low costs.

Third-party payers—for example private insurance, health-maintenance organizations (HMOs), managed care, and Medicare—provide benefits that make treatment possible, or at least less costly for many patients. Unhappily, some insurers introduce unnecessarily, burdensome complications for both patient and therapist. My practice is to tell prospective patients that our financial arrangements are directly between us. I will help with necessary forms and the providing of information, and they will deal with their insurer. In my experience, many insurers service their insurees in good faith, but some clearly do not, endlessly "losing" forms, claiming errors that don't exist, delaying payments, and demanding overly frequent treatment updates, unsuitable for long-term care.

Long-term care—psychoanalysis or psychotherapy—is expensive. For many people, the cost is accepted as a facet in the flow of monetary exchanges—education, vehicles, vacations, and hospitalizations—that characterize life. These prospective patients, alone or with their family, budget the expected cost in anticipation, without heightened distress. Other people may feel an immediate fear of exploitation and respond with oppositional self-interest. Details about sexual problems and intimate family secrets may be more easily revealed than facts about financial status, thereby making exploration of the financial aspect of the relationship impossible at the outset. Beyond the need to withhold information from others, a prohibition about revealing information about money may include not admitting to themselves or letting family members know, a practice that is followed in many well-to-do families with their grown children.

The discussion of fees brings the self-interests of patient and therapist into potential opposition. Polarities of greed and generosity, withholding and accommodating, rigidity and flexibility, inevitably play out in money (and other) negotiations. Issues that may require lengthy exploration during the treatment must be settled sufficiently to get the treatment underway. The patient has to divert money and time from other purposes, arrange transportation, deal with employers, or arrange babysitters. The patient can easily feel he gives the most, fills the therapist's open hours and pays for her lifestyle. The therapist is not a selfless participant in these exchanges. She does need her hours filled and the income to support choices for life satisfactions beyond those of her clinical work. Thus, patient and therapist are on equal footing as far as desires that derive from self-interest, but must be different in the way they manage their motivations. The therapist's professional discipline must operate as an intervening factor. What do I mean by professional discipline? The therapist's professional responsibilities include caring, stability, reliability, training, knowledge, sensitivity, dedication, and once again, caring—a commitment to put himself in the service of helping a patient. Paradoxically, however, if therapists were constituted only with these benevolent traits, they could not accomplish their therapeutic purposes. Therapists must have the capacity to sense into their own inclinations for greed, withholding, and rigidity to appreciate the place of these qualities in their patients' lives. Therapists must sense their own proclivities for problematic choices to explore those contexts during the treatment when negative attributes enter the exchange from either or both members of the dyad (chapter 6). A therapist's professional discipline refers to using knowledge of the self to monitor the byplay of contradictory desires while achieving the goals of the patient for a therapeutic outcome.

The patient's desire to be helped and the therapist's desire to help are both starting points for treatment and core motivations that sustain the treatment through its many strains.

A frequent source of strain arises from charges for missed sessions. As with the number and timing of appointments and the cost per session, many patients accept the therapist's proposal without rancor. For some patients, however, the prospect of being charged for missed sessions seems unbelievably unfair, if their work, vacation, illness, choice, or forgetting leads to their absence from a scheduled appointment. We do not generally expect to pay for services that have not been rendered or commodities we have not received. Alternatively, we do expect to pay rent or mortgage, or annual charges for a reserved tennis court even when we are away from our apartment, or house, or don't use the court. So with two distinct patterns for acceptable charge arrangements, therapists can select one, or the other, or a modification. My particular practice is to charge for missed appointments with two provisos: If I can fill the hour with a consultation, I will not charge; if I can arrange a substitute hour within the same week, I do so. If weather conditions make travel hazardous, I recommend we have the session by phone. Because many of my patients travel frequently, we try to work out maintaining the scheduled number of sessions by phone, often by being flexible about the timing of sessions. My goal is to maintain the continuity so necessary for effective exploration. To facilitate patients' planning, I furnish them with a list of times I am away four to six months in advance. Although I believe I can justify my policy as providing mutual benefit, I am fully aware that I am serving my self-interest in maintaining a steady income. Moreover, I found early in my career that getting into the position of judging the justification for a patient's absence interfered with the type of open listening that is integral to the "service" I am providing. My policy works for me as a person and with the type of practice I have, treating patients and supervising established colleagues and therapists-in-training over extended periods of time. Other policies employed by therapists include allowing a set number of cancellations or no charge for particular reasons or if notice of cancellation is made at a fixed time in advance.

"How long will the treatment take?" is a question that inevitably arises during the consultation, often explicitly, inevitably implicitly. And it can't be answered. To know how long a treatment, project, trip, or war will take conveys a sense of security, especially when costs and sacrifices are involved. Any final statement of time for an exploratory psychotherapy or psychoanalysis would convey a false safety. Even averages and statistics do not help. In my experience, the length of time I have worked with patients in psychotherapy has varied from months to many years and successfully completed analysis from four to twelve years. Less is lost in acknowledging that no real assessment is possible than an illusory gain from the intellectual dishonesty of offering to predict the unpredictable and setting up an unrealistic expectation. The essential problem is that the exploration proceeds optimally when an open-ended spirit of inquiry prevails. Open-ended does not mean being without goal or direction or an awareness of pragmatic considerations; rather open-ended means therapist and patient cocreate an ambiance that works against easy assumptions and premature shutting down of inquiry. Meaningful reassurance arises from a recognition that, throughout the treatment, remaining open-minded can guide the process of exploration, while both patient and therapist can attend the process and recognize indications that the treatment is moving toward an ending stage.

Can a patient benefit maximally from intensive psychotherapy and analysis and also receive the benefit of an additional form of help? How are the arrangements affected if the patient is receiving medication, group therapy, a 12-step program, or yoga, or is learning meditation? Fifty years ago, intensive psychotherapy, and especially psychoanalysis, was thought to be incompatible with other methods. Analysts then feared that, if symptoms were relieved, patients would lose the motivation to endure the emotional and financial costs of lengthy treatment. Further, analysts believed that if other helpers were involved in the patient's recovery, the transference experience would be split. The needed intensity would be reduced. Essential information would be scattered. Rivalries and jealousies would be set up and "acted out."

Experience for many analysts, and certainly for me, has not borne out these fears. Although symptoms may be the precipitants that bring some patients to seek and accept intensive psychotherapy, most patients recognize explicitly or implicitly that their problems lie more basically in their sense of self, their long-term patterns of personality. The essential source of therapeutic leverage arises from interlocking processes of an intersubjective relationship and an exploration of experience, meanings, and motives. What do I mean by interlocking processes? The answer lies in the particular duality of a therapeutic relationship and an investigative exploration. No matter how beneficial a therapist–patient relationship becomes, alone it will not lead to the desired changes, unless the motives, values, and goals that comprise a person's sense of self are explored, but motives and meanings cannot be explored unsupported by an essentially sustaining relationship. Moreover, a unique feature of intensive psychotherapies is that the shifting strains at the junction of a patient's and a therapist's communications create a relational experience, one that calls for definition and a comprehensible set of emotion-laden meanings. The relationship and the exploration interlock in that the shifting strains of the relationship provide crucial data from which the most significant aspects of understanding are derived.

Given this view of therapeutic leverage, medication and other means of relieving distress, adding understanding, and altering behavioral patterns, can provide background support, and often valuable information. My approach to medication is somewhat idiosyncratic. I believe to be an expert in the ever-increasing complexity of psychotropic medications is a specialty and art in itself. Therefore, I believe my patients are better served by having me refer them to colleagues who have that expertise. Additionally, my patients and I will not need to deviate from our exploratory effort to discuss adjustments in dosage and shifts in drug choices. Furthermore, the patient has contact with a colleague who can serve as a resource when I am unavailable.

This then leads to the presumed danger of splitting, diluting, or rivalry. I take the view that if my patient can be helped with his addiction by a 12-step program, her anxiety by meditation, his shyness and isolation by being in a therapy group, or her body tension and weight concerns by yoga or pilates, the added help will facilitate the sense of safety and hope needed to sustain a long-term psychotherapy. Therapeutic understanding benefits greatly from exploring the methods that patients employ to experience relief and vitality. As to rivalry and jealousy, where patients are consciously or unconsciously pulling their therapists into such roles by activating the potential of the therapists to be rivalrous or jealous, this becomes a fertile area for intersubjective recognition, self-inquiry by the therapists, and interpretive exploration with the patients.

Research in development describes how a child develops a sense of safety, and a person at any age creates and maintains security. Knowing that we have someone to whom we can turn at a time of danger and loss, someone who will comfort and restore, is basic. Likewise, the security of our attachments requires the experience of knowing that we are known, both to ourselves and to others, as the persons we deeply sense ourselves to be. Stated differently, we come into the world carried in the symbolic reality of our parents' minds and retain a sense of existence from experiences throughout life in the caring minds of others, as they exist reciprocally in ours. We gain confirmation of our positive value as our feelings, thoughts, and actions are mirrored, that is, recognized and affirmed. We feel safe in the kinship of like-minded others and in situations of mutual respect and admiration. Finally, the ability to communicate to others via words and gestures secures our conviction of the power to influence our destiny.

I began this chapter referring to establishing a therapeutic frame that facilitates an ambiance of safety. Therapists lay the foundation through friendliness, reliability, consistency, and a mutually arrived at, workable agreement on time and fee arrangements. In subsequent chapters, I describe techniques that enhance the sense of safety for both. In a successful consultation, the patient will already be turning to the therapist as a secure base at moments of distress. Some sense of feeling understood will have begun, and, along with it, the respect and admiration that sustains hope. In the same way, parents prepare a space in their minds for their baby-to-be, both patient and therapist begin a process of carrying an expanding mental version of the other, and of the two together, in all their varied and complex emotional interactions. In the next chapter, I describe how therapists gain critically needed understanding of their patients' needs, desires, intentions, emotions, and meanings through empathic listening.

CHAPTER 2

SENSING INTO THE MIND-STATES OF ANOTHER

EXPLORATORY PSYCHOTHERAPIES ARE BASED ON two happenings in the dyadic relationship of therapist and patient. First, the therapist attempts to gain an accurate understanding of the conscious and unconscious states of mind of the patient. Second, the patient inadvertently misunderstands the therapist and the therapeutic situation based on expectations drawn from his significant past experience. Both of these statements, although correct in their essentials, require explanation and emendation. I consider that the therapist's principal understanding arises from an empathic mode of perception or empathic listening. The patient's misunderstanding is considered as "transference." (I have much more to say about transference in chapter 6.) For now, I describe what I consider to be a therapist's fundamental task: the systematic application of the empathic mode of perception.

In the past, patients could be said to pay an expert in psychological processes to have their problems become known and resolved. Even if an omniscient expert could perform this feat, the patients would have been shortchanged. Patients, indeed all humans who enter into an intimate relationship, wish to be known not as a collection of psychopathology but as the person they are—past and present motives, intentions, feelings, attitudes, plans, goals, achievements, failures, values, loves, hates and some indefinable spark beyond. These comprise elements of what is to be discovered and explored for a patient to feel "known." How do therapists go about this search for a troubled patient's essential humanity? How do therapists help patients to overcome doubt, suspicion, shame, humiliation, embarrassment, fear, and guilt sufficiently for patients to reveal a sensitive aspect of their experiences? Therapists gain their critical information primarily by orienting their listening stance from within the perspective, the state of mind, of the patient. Listening from within the patient's perspective means perceiving and conceptualizing the whole context of how a patient is sensing himself, how he is sensing others, how he senses the source of his feelings and thoughts, and what he feels is the range of his potential solutions to his problems.

In 1967, Ralph Greenson described his use of this approach:

> I change the way I am listening to her. I shift from listening from the outside to listening from the inside. I have to let a part of me become the patient, and I have to go through her experiences as if I were the patient and to introspect what is going on in me as they occur. . . . I let myself experience the analytic hour, her associations, and her affects as she seems to have gone through them in the hour. I go back over the patient's utterances and transform her words into pictures and feelings in accordance with her personality. I let myself associate to these pictures with *her* life experiences, *her* memories, *and her* fantasies. As I have worked with this patient over the years I have built up a working model of the patient consisting of her physical appearance, her behavior, her ways of moving, her desires, feelings, defenses, values, attitudes, etc. It is this working model of the patient that I shift into the foreground as I try to capture what she was experiencing. The rest of me is de-emphasized and isolated for the time being [pp. 367–368].

The approach Greenson described varies in the difficulty a therapist encounters in following it with any particular patient or with the same patient at different times. Veronica, a young attractive professional, described being so upset when the senior partner yelled at her that she could hardly continue to think and wanted to stay in her office avoiding everyone. As she related details of their verbal interchange, I thought it unlikely that her soft-spoken, controlled senior partner had "yelled," but he had been critical when she had hoped for praise. Sensing the experience from her perspective, I could easily understand her portrayal of a critical comment as yelling and the reason she was undone by it. Veronica, when a graduate student, had begun treatment because of anxiety attacks following her calling home to get the name of the family auto insurance company to report a minor accident. As luck would have it, her mother was out and she got her father, who rarely answered the phone. He immediately started screaming that she had never learned to drive properly, that she was always doing foolish things, and that he didn't need her to upset him. Over many subsequent sessions, Veronica described many other incidents of her father's frightening, angry outbursts and of his fragility, his inability to tolerate the least upset to his plans or routine. He would come to Veronica's athletic events, and if she made what he thought was a mistake or a poor play, she would hear his voice screaming at her over the din of the other sounds. From knowledge of these experiences, I could readily understand from her vantage point how the criticism of the senior partner was experienced as a mind-shattering yell.

Veronica made several unsuccessful forays into love affairs with men. These left her bereft, frightened, and pessimistic about the future in ways into which I could more or less easily sense. After the breakup with Phil, however, a romance that had seemed to have greater promise, she became inconsolably obsessed with the idea that Phil must come back, he must call and explain, he must see her and talk to her. From every description of their ending, his dropping of her without explanation and his subsequent pointed avoidance of her, I regarded as unlikely his complying with her mandatory demand. Positioning myself as a sympathetic observer, offering her evidence for my doubting that he would come back, did nothing to soften her insistence, and only increased her anger at me, and the intensity of her obsessive reiterations. We, each of us, had contributed to, cocreated, a stalemate. My recognition of our stalemate opened me to the further recognition that I had lost my observational stance as an empathic listener and then could not regain it effectively with the information I had access to. I knew that for Veronica, my reliability in returning her calls, either when she was upset or needed to reschedule a session, was of greater than usual importance in the security she felt with me. Yet still he *must* come to her and explain? I described my dilemma to Veronica, and the tone of our interchanges improved. Over the next several weeks, from dreams and associations, we could appreciate the significance not only of her battles with her father that we had already considered in detail, but of their then making up, a sequence that was now newly available to us. After being screamed at, Veronica might fight back for a while, appeal to her mother with little effect, and eventually withdraw into a hurt, sulky dissociative state until her father would come to her room. He would tell her he didn't mean it, he loved her, and would woo her back into a good mood, calling her by his pet names for her.

Once these memories emerged, I could appreciate from Veronica's perspective that Phil must come back because she had relied on father's coming to her room to reinstate her connectedness to him and help her to break out of a dissociative state. These making-up moments encapsulated a core experience of romantic attachment and a compensation for mistreatment. As we worked further with the making-up scene, I could see, and help her to see, she also concluded from it that she was more important to her father than her mother was to him because mother did not get this same postfight wooing. In addition Veronica recognized the trap this placed her in; father's actions did not reflect authentic regret, but his self-serving, openly acknowledged need for her smiling face to put him at ease. With this understanding, we could appreciate the central wound of Phil's not coming back. It meant he didn't need her smiles or interest at all. This constituted a powerful blow to a major source of her self-value. These experiences with Veronica illustrate that empathic perception, when present, enables analytic understanding to move forward and, when absent, alerts an analyst to a problem that must be addressed. When empathic listening can be restored, fresh efforts to gain a new perspective by therapist and patient are generally rewarded by significant progress.

EMPATHY AND SYMPATHY

Empathy, when not specified as a mode of perception, is often confused with sympathy. Sensing into the state of mind of a troubled patient will often enhance the possibility of sympathy such as I could feel for Veronica's becoming distraught by, in her perception, being yelled at by the senior partner. Empathic perception, however, is essentially value-free. A person sensing how another experiences the world around can use that information to exploit or injure, as well as to open channels for communication and exploration. Kohut gave the example that the Nazi air force, recognizing the fearful state of mind that screaming dive-bombers could induce, equipped *Stukas* with sirens. Con artists and imposters are masters of using empathic perception to dupe and victimize. Nonetheless, in a treatment situation, empathic listening is often connected to sympathy. By this I refer not only to the sympathy a therapist may feel for his patient's plight, but also the sympathy a patient may feel for himself as he understands his experiences more completely. For Veronica to appreciate that her obsessional demand "he must come back" derived from significant past experiences permitted her to believe herself to be a person whose symptomatic demands had meaning, rather than regarding herself as foolishly immature. Shame was replaced by understanding; depression by disappointment and regret. My success in finally being able to sense into and interpret to her her state of mind opened to her the opportunity to be an empathic perceiver of herself. Her humiliation could give way to self-sympathy.

Strictly speaking, the empathic mode of perception is a mode of investigation. As a principle of technique, empathic listening is central to the inquiry needed for the therapist to obtain essential knowledge of the patient's inner world. The effects of a therapist's empathic listening transcend data gathering, however. A therapist's persistent effort to know how a patient is sensing himself and others earns the therapist a special place in the patient's life. A sense of being known, of having her dreams, feelings, attitudes, goals, and values treated seriously has a vitalizing effect over and above the explicit knowledge of the specific meanings arrived at through empathic perception. Moreover, as patients ponder their therapists' communications about their states of mind, they activate their own introspective capacities. Empathic listening by therapists provides a model for patients to sense their troubling motivations more deeply and with less fright. Along with greater perceptiveness about themselves, patients generally become more able to see others in a broader perspective, others being parents, spouses, friends, children, and the therapist.

HOW DOES THE ABILITY TO SENSE INTO THE STATES OF MIND OF ANOTHER DEVELOP?

Life begins for all of us with a caregiver trying to sense into our states of mind, trying to make an educated guess about our emotional states, our needs, and our intentions. Do we want to be fed or have our diaper changed? Do we want to be played with and stimulated, or left alone to explore or get drowsy? Are we frowning and angry about something, and if so, what is it? When our smile turned to fright, was it the loud noise that startled, or the unfamiliar person who walked in? Is it this toy or that one we are reaching for? Do we want to be picked up or left to crawl?

Hundreds of times each day in the life of an infant, a caregiver matches smiles with a baby's smiles and gives touches of ironic matches of anger or fear or sadness that tell a baby she knows how he feels and that it isn't really so bad. Or it *is* so bad, and hunger won't be allowed to go on too much longer.

A caregiver is sensing into her baby's immediate and general state of mind to regulate the baby's state and provide for the baby's needs, not to inform the baby about her state. Yet in fact, caregivers are constantly interpreting a baby's state to her. "Oh, I see you are hungry." Or, "OK, you have had enough." Or, "What an ugly diaper; no wonder you were crying." Or, "You want your blanky over here so you can go to sleep." Sometimes a caregiver's "chatter" is a statement, and sometimes it is a question; but the result is that a baby is introduced into a process through which mind-states are appreciated from visual, auditory, facial, and gestural clues long before the words used to describe and explain the findings are meaningful to the baby. Of course, a mother's empathic perceptivity will equip her to be more or less able to sense how her baby's communications and his temperament, or her own early life experiences and unconscious patterns of procedural memory, are pulling her one way or another.

How does an infant and toddler come to appreciate a mind-state, whether his caregiver's or his own? Emotion is central. Her face, his face—they match configurations in thousands of communicative and care-taking exchanges until, at about 10 months of age, an infant intentionally looks at his mother's face to read her emotion and gestures to gain guidance from it. If she points, his eyes will follow the direction indicated rather than focus on her hand as an object of interest, and he will also use his finger as a pointer in a situation of uncertainty and ambiguity. If she looks encouraging, he will proceed; if she looks frightened, he will stop. If he smiles at her and she gives a blank-face response, he will try harder to get the smile he expects, and if her face remains blank, he will be disconcerted, distressed, and turn away. All of these communicative exchanges establish patterns of interaction of self with other in the form of brain schemas, "scenes," or "maps." These experiences are categorized and encoded in memory in increasing complexity of interconnections with other experiences. These early schemas of how the developing self gets on with others, and especially the emotions involved, form the basis for a capacity for empathic perception after many more developmental milestones have been passed.

Around 18 to 24 months (sometimes earlier) a toddler develops the capacity to think using symbols. Words, phrases, and sentences become the tools to tell others and oneself what one wants and feels and what is going on with others. Play enters a new phase in which objects are no longer interesting only for their properties, their colors, the noise they make, and the textures they have, but for their usefulness in pretend games. A stick can become an imaginary spoon for a pretend game of feeding a doll, or it can become an imaginary weapon to go "bang bang" with. All of this provides toddlers with an increasing refinement of knowledge of their intentions. Then, beginning at around 24 months, they will experiment with the power of directed opposition, of saying "no," even to something they want, to enforce a sense of self against other, a sense of oppositional agency. Toddlers know that the minds of others can provide signals to orient them and can be either like-minded in intention or oppositional in conflicting agendas. This is not the same as being able to be other-minded, to be able to sense or imagine into the mind of another.

At this stage, a toddler simply perceives the world through her own eyes, ears, and thought processes and cannot imagine another view exists. A child sitting on one side of a table automatically assumes her brother on the other side is having the same experiences as she is. If an object is taken from her view and placed so she can't see it but he can, she cannot de-center from her own view to adopt his view.

Until the age of five or six, children are limited in their ability to recognize and appraise the state of mind of another. Three- and four-year-olds believe in the veridicality of their thoughts and often what they are told. This renders them gullible to the implausible lies of others and themselves, such as the chair threw the book down or a ghost broke the glass. At five or six, they would assign such misdeeds more accurately to the perpetrator. Another limitation on sensing into the mind of another is the three- or four-year-old's inability to distinguish between an intention and a desire. If the child intends to build a Lego house, he may be equally satisfied if he builds it himself or if someone builds it for him; his intention to build and his desire to have are indistinguishable. At five or six, he may become frustrated if his intention to build is not allowed to proceed. He recognizes that his intention to build something himself is a different motive than a desire to possess an already-built object.

Another critical factor in developing empathic perception of others and oneself is the ability to recognize that what a person thinks, indeed, is certain of, may still be wrong. What looks like one thing may turn out to be another, and someone else seeing it may make the same mistake. To look at the world through the eyes of another must include both an appreciation that an empathic perceiver can often make an accurate enough assessment and recognition that one's intuition or appraisal may be askew or incorrect.

From the beginning of life, infants track contingencies. They build patterns and derive expectations from observing and categorizing the sequences: if B follows A, then A caused B. The possibility of arriving at a false conclusion by a child is increased by conflating cause with intent and desire. A child of four who was eagerly looking forward to going to the zoo the next day was told by his father, "Don't get your hopes up; it will probably rain." When he awoke to a heavy rain, he thought his father caused the rain because his father didn't want him to go; he wanted to punish him for breaking his new toy. The child's assumption about his being punished for breaking the toy was based on a belief in his father's omniscience and omnipotence rather than the father's actual knowledge or power. This example combines the dual problem of children's teleological reasoning and magical thinking. Both of these tendencies tend to persist in later life and interfere with empathic perception.

Much observation and research emphasizes caregiver–child interactions for establishing the development of a concept of how oneself and others think and feel. Sometimes this cognitive emphasis overlooks the very serious business of play: play with parents, play alone in the shadow of others, play with toys, pretend play with imaginary others, and especially play with peers. Play gives a child an opportunity to test out her own inventiveness and, in peer play, to contrast with others. Peer play opens children to the parameters of pretend and real, of an intended hit and an accidental one, of anger and making up, of testing one child's appraisal of another's state of mind, of how an appraisal made about oneself and others can be wrong. All of this contributes to the child's forming a workable theory of how minds function and opens the way to empathic perception.

The significance of play cannot be appreciated from activities and interactions alone, however. Play's most salient feature is the affect of playfulness. Playfulness offers a sense of safety to toy with ideas, to puzzle over ambiguities and paradoxes. Playfulness, humor, irony, and satire create a spirit that both breaks down barriers people put up about their mind-states and allows for a nonthreatening entry into that state. Not surprisingly, dream interpretation, spontaneity of association, and many moments of successful empathic perception flourish when a spirit of play is present.

For a long time, the developmental steps that allow an older child, adolescent, and adult to make more accurate assessments of their own state of mind and that of others were considered largely products of the maturation of the individual's brain. We now recognize the strong influence of the caregiver–child relationship on the brain systems. Fifty-seven infant–mother pairs were evaluated when the infants were six months old. The children at four years of age who demonstrated the highest capacity for a workable theory of how minds work were the children whose mothers used language that commented appropriately on their infant's mental state. "Oh you're hungry." "You want me to play with you." "You want your blanky." "I love, love, love your smile." Not surprisingly, the child's own verbal ability predicted success in understanding mental experience. Systems of the brain, language, and empathic ability are all interrelated with caregiver–child experience.

A child's developing an ability to sense mind-states of others will be compromised by caregivers whose face and gestures convey anger, fear, depression, shame, and a blank absence of emotion, those who do not notice or communicate about the child's mental state, or those who use mental state language but consistently misidentify their baby's needs and intentions. Consequently, relationships that are communicative and communications that are based on accurate identifications of desires and intentions contribute to the development of a capacity for reflectively thinking about one's own thinking and for appraising the mental state of others. Recognition of the developmental power of an open communicative relationship supports a conviction that successful exploratory therapy will further enhance a patient's reflective and appraisal capacities.

LISTENING FROM WITHIN, LISTENING FROM OUTSIDE, AND BUILDING AN "OBSERVATIONAL PLATFORM"

We do not ordinarily attempt systematically and persistently to sense into another person's states of mind or, for that matter, into our own. More commonly, we take the position of an outside observer, the stance that science in the past has extolled for its objectivity in comparison to the suspect subjectivity of empathic listening. We are no longer convinced, however, of the objectivity of an outside observer (the observer cannot be removed from what is observed) and are no longer as doubtful of empathic listening. Each listening stance has its merits. Therapists inevitably shift back and forth between them. The observer's listening stance enables therapists to recognize, identify, and interpret patterns as they emerge, thereby providing a broader view of their interactions than a patient is likely to recognize. The observer stance helps to counter a tendency therapists might have to limit their observations and comments to being sympathetic or soothing when straight talk and confrontation may better serve to move the inquiry forward. The empathic mode of perception facilitates therapists' understanding of the timing, meaning, and motivation involved in patients' states, from expansive to deflated and depressed, from idealizing to depreciating, from dominating to submissive. Empathic listening enhances therapists' skill in sensing, identifying, and giving coherence to altered, dissociated mood and bodily states that patients frequently experience, especially patients who have suffered severe trauma. When a therapist is positioned as an observer, remaining in touch with patients during mind and body state transitions and sensing their immediate or remote origin is more difficult.

I have found that systematically listening from within the frame of reference of patients' feelings and thoughts often enables therapists to observe and interpret in a manner that permits therapist and patient to construct an "observational platform" on which both can stand. Sharing an observational stance together, each can bring forward associations to a dream, to an event, to how each is sensing the other, and to what is and has been transpiring between them. Therapists at these moments are able to make rapid shifts in their vantage point to avail themselves of the benefits each listening stance offers as a source of information gathering and appreciation of meaning. Therapist or patient may visualize an affectively charged interaction between the patient and others, with shifting empathic perception of each party. Therapist or patient may visualize an emotionally charged interaction between them that gives to their experience during the sessions a sense of tension or calm, dullness or liveliness, irritability or friendliness, sexual excitement or affection. The therapist may let her attention fall on how the patient is experiencing her. The therapist's quickly oscillating attentiveness may shift to her own responses to their shared closeness. Is it comfortable for her, charged with excitement or smugness, or too precarious to maintain? Are they each feeling the same, or is the emotion and attitude confined to one or the other? When the treatment has progressed and both are experiencing a comfortable moment on the observational platform, a therapist may suddenly envision a whole vista of the experience of the session, the prior sessions, and their prior understandings of the past. From this vista, the analyst and the patient may arrive at a new set of integrations. The mind play between therapist and patient at these moments can reveal a developed joint capacity for utilizing the empathic perception of the other and of the intersubjective field between them.

CLINICAL EXAMPLE

Mr. Black began two-sessions-per-week therapy after his wife, Barbara, discovered he secretly remained in correspondence with the lover he had had in college. Having completed a postgraduate degree, Mr. Black was now beginning a successful professional career. Mr. Black came faithfully to sessions and filled the time with detailed chronicles of phone calls to his family or conversations with Barbara and others. The striking feature of his discourse was cynical skepticism, the only feeling present. Intermittently he would refer to his college lover with implications of mourning for the closeness they had had and the follower role he had fallen into then. Now at his work and with Barbara, he had become more of a leader. He responded with evident relief to my seeing through his eyes that he was painfully disappointed with his family's values. Growing up he had admired his father's entrepreneurial endeavors and his mother's optimism. Then, during late adolescence, he became disillusioned, and he built a wall of skepticism. With each detailed rendering of a conversation with a family member, I tried to identify and interpret the immediate source of the disillusion he was expressing in his skeptical style. Sometimes cynicism was triggered by his father's controlling obsessive preoccupation with logistics. Sarcasm was his response to his mother's insistence that she would listen only to good news. In another conversation, his skeptical wall went up when his father would try to sell him on the great prospects of a deal Mr. Black was certain would never come off. At other times the "foolishness" of people he worked with set him off. By staying within his perspective, I was able to help him to realize that his love affair during college had helped him to fill the gaps in his life that resulted from the traumatic disillusion with and withdrawal from his family. His intimacy with Barbara became more consolidated, and his wall of skepticism sufficiently diminished for them to plan a family. The session I describe occurred as his wife's pregnancy was late in the third trimester.

PATIENT: I want to tell you about a visit we made to friends who are about as pregnant as we are. They showed us the nursery they have prepared. They were so taken with all of it, the changing table and all the baby clothes. I knew they would ask about our preparations and I wasn't sure how I would handle our not having anything yet. Same with my in-laws and my mother—when are you going to buy something? We will, but what's the big deal? It's just stuff, and we'll have it when we need it.
THERAPIST: It comes across to you as people putting all the emphasis on stuff, equipment, being materialistic, and arousing your skepticism.

PATIENT: Yes, I get cynical when my mother asks what we bought or what she should buy, but does not ask how Barbara is.
THERAPIST: You feel concerns that the well-being of people gets lost.

PATIENT: And I don't like the pressure. The more Barbara and I hear from our families, the more we are in no hurry.
THERAPIST: You are more inclined to dig in your heels.

PATIENT: When our friends were showing us all the things they bought, I couldn't help looking at Barbara and smiling.
THERAPIST: You took a cynical view of their pride.

PATIENT: They did seem to be enjoying it, but I kept thinking how ridiculous all this is. Does anybody need all that? I know we will get a changing table, crib, and stroller. Not yet.
THERAPIST: They were taking pleasure in their preparations, and you were enjoying something different. You enjoy refusing to go along a conventional timing and focus, smiling at the people who do.

PATIENT: People like my father who have to order tickets months in advance and plan everything to the last detail and still get the big things messed up. [He then talked about Barbara and her mother, who like to do things sparsely. Barbara remembered her mother told her she was changed on a bed. They were unsure whether they needed a crib or would keep the baby in their room. He then returned to the visit and talk with the friends. As he spoke, in my mind's eye I began to picture looking at a changing table and a crib with the pleasure of anticipating a baby using them. Something in Mr. Black's tone suggested that he was less caught up in defensive, resistant cynicism, and the ambiance had changed to a more relaxed acceptance. Consequently, I felt free to offer an interpretation both from an empathic stance within his perspective and from my own perspective as an observer.]
THERAPIST: So you clearly gain a feeling of superiority and freedom from your rebellious stand against convention and the pressure to be preoccupied with logistics, goods, and overabundance. But do you sacrifice the pleasure you imply your friends are gaining from picturing their baby in a room, lovingly prepared for him or her?

PATIENT: I don't know. [Long thoughtful pause.] I just remembered Barbara's mother sent us a snowsuit for the baby. It was lying out on the bed. It is little, and with the hood and all, it looked like a baby. I was a little startled, and I had the thought, "Oh, that will be the baby." So for the minute I did anticipate [in a tone of warmth].
THERAPIST [reflecting this was a rare moment of Mr. Black's spontaneously associating to an affective moment free of his

wall of skepticism]: And you felt open to enjoying the prospect—a live little baby.

PATIENT: And I told Barbara, and we laughed.

This small vignette reveals the utilization of the empathic mode of perception in an intensive psychotherapy. Concern has been voiced that systematically trying to perceive a patient's experiences from his perspective will merely confirm that view, lock the patient into it, and render him dependent on the therapist for support. My experience does not confirm any of these dire predictions. Patients like Mr. Black recognize that I am struggling along with them to identify and verbalize their point of view, that I am not indicating that I do or don't share it or believe it is or is not an accurate inference to draw. Empathic listening conveys that communications such as Mr. Black's filter of skepticism can be understood from inferences he has made from his lived experience. By approaching many instances of the immediate origins of his cynicism, we could gradually piece together a larger portrayal. Mr. Black as a little boy fully accepted his family's myths of riches to come, false optimism based on denial, and secretive denial of their ethnic origin. For his compliance, he won their approval as the good child in the family. In adolescence, as he emerged from his idealization, he fell into another "enchantment" with his lover. He emerged with a protective shield of disbelief, including a disbelief in any of his positive emotions. As Mr. Black could understand the present version of what his skepticism was designed to block out, imperceptibly he began to feel safe enough to admit more varied affective experiences. As he began to understand the earlier origins of his need for cynicism, he could feel safe enough to be open to an alternative, more positive orientation. The more positive orientation that occurred in this session was his openness to the pleasure of anticipation of his baby-to-be. Rather than being locked into a limited perspective by my sensing into his skepticism, Mr. Black became free to recognize and acknowledge an alternative feeling. The therapist's shifting focus of attention facilitates the entire therapeutic process.

I have described the significance of my primary focus on Mr. Black's perspective as seen from his point of view, present and past. Similarly, my attention turned to the picture I formed of what was happening as he returned to describing his friends' proud display of their newly set-up nursery. I used my own construction (and experience) to infer their pleasure in anticipating the coming baby and recognize the specific cost to Mr. Black of the pleasure of his cynical oppositional stance. To my primary focus on Mr. Black's perspective and the secondary focus on my own vision, I added a third focus on the state of relations between us. I used my focus on the state of relations between us, as well as the ambiance of the moment that we had created, to determine the content and timing of my intervention. Obviously, this third focus is not arrived at by labored linear thinking but by intuitive feel. From my intuitive appraisal, I concluded Mr. Black had become far more in touch with his feelings over many sessions and progressively more so as this session progressed. We seemed to be working well together as he acknowledged the pleasure he felt in being oppositional. Something in his telling about the friends in the nursery suggested to me that my vision might not be foreign to him. Sensing a subtlety in our communication that I was willing to trust, I suggested the alternative of pleasure in anticipating the baby's presence. The state between us thus provided a guide for my use of a dual focus of sensing into his mind and looking into my own.

The clinical examples I have presented illustrate that a therapist's sensing into the mind of a patient is central to an exploratory therapy. Sensing the viewpoints and experiences of a patient requires sensitive listening to the full range of the patient's communications combined with information gained through the therapist's introspection. In the next chapter I will describe the significance of emotions to facilitate therapists' entry into patients' experiences and intentions.

CHAPTER 3

AFFECTS AND THE PATHWAY TO MOTIVATION

MANY YEARS AGO WHEN I WAS PUZZLED by the actions and symptoms of very disturbed patients, my mentor, Lewis Hill, told me that people only do things that make sense to them from the point of view that they hold. The task of a therapist is to find that point of view, even if the patient doesn't know or remember it. Finding the point of view of patients begins with recognizing their emotional experiences. Finding the sense their symptoms or actions make to them requires that we discover the affective goal patients seek and thereby understand their motivations. This chapter describes techniques designed to aid in the discovery of affective experiences associated with often puzzling motivations.

Emotions or affects (I use the terms interchangeably) may be subtle, like the contempt demonstrable in a raised eyebrow or so suppressed as to be invisible to self or observer. Or emotions may be as striking as the full-faced smile of joy and laughter or the contorted face of anger and fear. Emotions may be as fleeting as a momentary regret, as lasting as a mood of sadness, or as all-consuming as a serious depression.

In clinical exchanges, therapists seek answers to two questions about emotion. The first, and generally easier to answer, is the nature of a patient's affect during an experience he is describing. Whether he is relating a dream or referring to an experience with the analyst during a previous session or to an event in his daily life, the emotion or emotions he experiences while going through it must be known to appreciate the significance and meaning of the event to him. The affect experienced during the event may be included fully in the description or may be relatively easily accessible in response to a therapist's question. Or the affect experienced during the event, say, romantic longings in the dream or an angry criticism in the prior session, may be hidden behind shame, guilt, or fear. The affect being experienced immediately, whether shame, fear, or guilt, must be understood and articulated first before the affect experienced during the event can be accessed. The affects I am referring to may be either conscious or easily brought into awareness through inquiry.

A striking feature of success in reexperiencing an emotion during the relating of it is that patients hear themselves telling the therapist about it. Consequently the emotion and the context in which it originated become more sharply delineated. Therapists' interest, helpful questions, and mirroring responses enable patients not only to hear themselves, but also to listen to themselves empathically. The spirit of inquiry that informs their dialogue opens the recognition of affective experience into more than simply living it or reliving it; the way is open to *reflect* on it. Now therapist and patient, each alone and together, widen their perspective and deepen their understanding of the patient's experience.

When relating an experience, patients tend to remember emotions that arose during the event and those that followed, that is, a happy or unhappy outcome. A patient related that he was happy when he first arrived at his parents' home for Christmas, but then the old disagreements surfaced. He left wondering why he went, and he still wonders. To help explore his question, we need to ask, what was the affect he sought in making his decision to go? In this instance, the answer was relatively easily obtained. He was motivated by a hope that he would be welcomed and cherished and that he could recapture some of the childhood magic of Christmas. He added that now that he could recognize the expectation on which his decision had been made, he no longer was tormenting himself for being so foolish. He added he didn't think he would be so unguarded again. The point I am trying to make is that therapists ask two different questions about emotions. One question, what was the affect experienced during and following an event, enables the therapist to enter into the patient's feeling state. The second question, what was the affect and goal the patient sought when acting in a certain way, enables both therapist and patient to explore the patient's motivation.

The answer to both questions would be the same at those times when the affect that had been experienced and the affect that had been sought coincide. A patient may say, "I went to the musical to be amused and delighted, and I most certainly was." Sometimes, the discrepancy is easily recognized: "I had another awful phone call to my mother. I started out being conciliatory and hoped she'd appreciate it, that we could get out of the cycle of blaming we are in, but it didn't happen." Frequently, however, the affect and goal being sought is not recognized or considered, and even if it is, it may be difficult to discern as in several of the examples that follow.

Benjamin, a bright, conscientious graduate student, arrived for his session in a state of distress. He announced that he had just had proof of how self-destructive he was. He was certain he had done poorly on a midterm test, or at least not as well as he might have done. His critical father had questioned whether he belonged in so prestigious a school, and he believed he must have been proving him right. Maybe, he wondered, he was simply bent on failing, and the analysis wouldn't help. I invited him to tell me what had happened during the exam. He described feeling groggy and having a hard time concentrating. He really knew the material, but his attention would flag as he tried to develop his answers more fully. He was seriously lacking in his usual spark. Picking up on his feeling groggy, I asked about his preparation. Well, he was embarrassed to say, he had pulled a virtual all-nighter as he had in college and used caffeine meds to stay awake, adding that such behavior proved to him that he intended to screw up.

I asked about his reverting to a pattern of all-nighters he had used in college. Looking back, he thought it had to do with his studying with George, a highly competitive classmate. George kept bringing up esoteric issues that he asserted had been on previous exams. Recognizing George's tendency to be a super-confident know-it-all who enjoyed triggering anxiety, Benjamin tried unsuccessfully to reason with himself. Instead of a brief review and a good night's sleep as he had planned, he began anxiously to over study, rationalizing that he might need to know detail after detail. The affect he was experiencing was anxiety; the affect he sought was confidence. His motive was not to prove his father's criticism correct, but to prove that his father was wrong and that he did indeed belong in a challenging program. This was the same goal John had formed at the dinner table growing up as he tried desperately to absorb information to be able to answer his father's nightly quizzes. In his pessimistic assumption that he sought failure and humiliation through a motive of masochistic self-destructiveness, he was demonstrating the teleological reasoning of young children. In the early stages of developing an understanding of human motivation and intentionality, children assume that the consequences or effect of a person's actions is a direct expression of the intention motivating the behavior. Consequently effect and intention are conceived as related in a linear and confused way. A child may think, "I'm unhappy since Mommy went to work. She must want me to be unhappy 'cause she doesn't like me or 'cause I'm bad." Or, "Mommy was crying when I came home. I must have made her cry." Children require the assistance of their attachment figures to help them develop their understanding of intentionality to be able to reflect effectively on their own motives and the motives of others. When patients remain locked into teleological thinking, as with Benjamin, the therapeutic dialogue provides an opportunity to acquire new understanding of why he and others do what they do.

Therapeutic consideration of examples like this helped Benjamin and his therapist to identify the affects and motivational goals he sought and the problems he had in achieving them. Benjamin learned that he had a problem regulating anxiety, that in competitive situations with peers he would lose his plans through destabilizing envy. He also learned that feelings of efficacy and confidence were evaluated by a worthy accomplishment, not by satisfying a hypercritical authority. The therapeutic inquiry began with conscious experiences of self-loathing and condemnation and proceeded to a discovery of anxiety about failure stirred by envy. The affects being sought were those of efficacy and confidence and praise from an idealized authority.

Recognition of the affect and goal being sought is particularly important in the treatment of patients with addictive and compulsive behaviors. Confusing the harmful effect of substance abuse, eating disorders, gambling, sexual enactments, self-cutting, and tongue biting with the conscious or unconscious affect being sought leaves a therapist limited to generally ineffective appeals to the patient's better judgment. Patients are often all too willing to use the fallacious reasoning that outcome indicates intent and rail at themselves for their stupidity in "doing it again," exacerbating their already debilitating shame.

The patient I now describe is an example of a person whose compulsive behavior could not be explored without understanding the affect being sought.

John, a businessman in his late 20s, worked as a manager in his father-in-law's company. His wife's family disapproved of the marriage, and after the birth of their daughter, his wife, as he put it, turned on him with the same disdain as her parents. He would do what he could to please her, and they would have good times. Inevitably, he would fail in her eyes, and her spiteful comments would leave him frustrated, his palliative apologies ineffectual. Feeling horrible, he would make up some excuse and get into his expensive car and head for the pick up area for male prostitutes. At first he withheld mention of his cruising from the treatment. Then he "confessed" with a barrage of self-hate and self-condemning name-calling. My interventions were of necessity limited to acknowledging his intense shame and humiliation. In time, he felt safe enough to allow us to track his affects, beginning with his humiliation at the hands of his wife and his willingness to side with her against himself, based on shame connected with his homosexual longings. She said he wasn't a real man, and he was enormously vulnerable to that accusation. Then his anger mounted, and with a mix of rage, defiance, and a degree of dissociation, he "found" himself "cruising" to make his pickup. For a time in our exploration, he insisted that all he wanted was a blowjob so he could have an orgasm and get over being horny. This he stated with defiance, annoyance, and a clear desire to put off further inquiry. Using dream material, feelings toward me, and more details of sensual caressing with the prostitute partners, however, he acknowledged that what he craved was the feeling someone wanted him and regarded his body as desirable. Then we could discuss his positive desires for intimacy and attachment, with the sensual component of loving touch. The recognition of the positive affects being sought allowed us to begin exploring the background for his strategy of seeking an attachment experience in the addictive, problematic manner to which he resorted.

The unusual clinical experience I now describe acted in a fashion that led to considerable puzzlement as to the emotion he was seeking. Larry, an unmarried, midlevel government employee, felt generally unsatisfied with his life. He described his activities as leaving him feeling flat. Emotionally, he was subdued, although to my judgment, not depressed. Gambling was the only activity that he described with interest and enthusiasm. He was in a regular poker game with relatively high stakes for his income. Sometimes he won, but often he lost, triggering more alarm for me than for him. On one occasion, he came to his morning session looking disheveled (very unusual for him) and stated he had been up all night. A most remarkable thing had happened. He had lost everything. He was cleaned out. He named an amount he had lost that really startled me.

Here we were. He was elated, and I was ready to throttle him. Unable to enter an empathic listening stance, I remonstrated, "How could you let yourself risk so much?" In my mind, concern for him was mixed with my self-interested worry that he was risking his continuing in the therapy. He was somewhat sobered by my expostulation, but, sticking to his guns, he said he didn't see it that way. He had waited for it to happen, he had expected it to happen, and now it had finally happened. He lost everything. He was cleaned out. As I returned to my listening stance, I tried to consider what affect he sought that he felt so pleased to have arrived at. I first considered it to be relief in that he had felt some awful occurrence was to befall him, and now that the sword of Damocles had fallen, he was relieved. Then I found myself resonating with the inflection of specialness he had given to the twice repeated, "I was cleaned out." I remembered that shortly after birth, he had been misdiagnosed as having coeliac syndrome, an often fatal disease of the pancreas that adversely affects the intestinal function of infants, with painful buildup of gas. He had, in fact, had an intolerance to milk, which can produce similar symptoms. His parents were concerned that he would die, and great anxiety surrounded his bowel functioning. To lose everything, to be all cleaned out, would mean that his painful abdominal distention was relieved, a source of elation to him and to his parents. It was as if he had come in to say to me, "Aren't you glad that I finally got cleaned out and that we can both feel the relief we have so often sought in vain?"

A focus on affective experiences places us in the realm of phenomenology, a careful delineation of the ebb and flow of mental processes. A focus on the affective experience being sought places us in the realm of needs, desires, goals, and intentions, or, more broadly, of motivation.

AFFECTS AND MOTIVATION

The link between emotions and motives begins early in life. To appreciate this early and fundamental linkage, we must consider motivation differently from the usual view. For older toddlers, children, adolescents, and adults, we regard motivation as meaning needs, desires, and intentions that are, or are able to be, organized symbolically into patterns of thoughts, dreams, and conscious or unconscious plans of action. Emotions provide the experiential salience and meaning to our thoughts and actions, that is, to the playing out of our motivations. Emotions provide the tonal qualities of our life, whether vital and joyous, calm and soothing, exciting and upbeat, confident and proud, dull and dreary, anxious and worrisome, angry and vengeful, shame-filled and downcast, embarrassed and shy, pain-filled and subdued, depressed and devitalized.

For a long time emotions were accorded a secondary position in psychoanalytic theories. They were viewed as by-products or derivations of drives, which were considered the central feature of conscious and especially unconscious motivation. The psychoanalytic theory of motivation can be said to have begun with Freud's recognition of the existence of sexuality in children and then evolved in a dizzying series of claims and counterclaims. At the beginning of the 20th century and continuing to the present, popular imagination was captured by the discovery that infants experienced erotic sensations and pleasure from sucking, bowel passage, and touch, especially genital fondling, and, at four or five years, had romantic fantasies about the parent of the opposite sex and rivalry with the parent of the same sex. Other theorists saw humans in quest of power and the intention to overcome inferiority. Encounters with war neuroses in World War I led to an emphasis on aggression or destructiveness as a motivational drive. Other studies by Freud, such as the biography of Leonardo da Vinci and the account of Schreber's psychotic grandiosity, brought in the motivational power of self-love or narcissism. Reaching a philosophic level, Freud postulated a life force or Eros in perpetual conflict with a death instinct or Thanatos. For many theorists, human relatedness came about only secondarily to recognizing that others—caregivers—were necessary to provide nutrient and other needs. In other theories, human relatedness was secondary to the presumed need of infants to rid them of the destructive force of a death instinct. In other theories, human relatedness was a primary motivational force, either simply "object" seeking or sought to provide a secure base at times of danger and loss. Other theorists have placed at the center of motivation the pursuit of mastery and efficacy, the need for safety, or the formation and maintenance of self-cohesion. As classical Freudian theory evolved, motivational significance was accorded not only to the sexual and aggressive drives, but also to an executive apparatus (the ego) and to an organization of ethical and moral injunctions and ideals (the superego). Affects played a particular role in the functioning of the apparatus in that unconscious anxiety alerted the executive agency to a potential danger, whereas unconscious guilt alerted it to a violation of morals. Other theorists added depression as alerting to a danger that had already occurred and shame as indicating a violation of ideals. Some theorists hypothesized that the motivational force they espouse arises from within the psyche of an individuated person, playing out against well-differentiated others. In recent years, an increasing number of other theorists have come to picture the motivations of each individual as consciously and unconsciously dependent on mutual influencing. This latter portrayal of motivation, with which I agree, holds that the affective life of child and caregiver, of adult and all significant others, and of therapist and patient, is influenced by and influences the other. In any particular interaction, the extent of influence of one partner on the other may shift at any moment. In my view, we can retain a view of psychic processes as emphasized by Freud along with mutual influence in that, at all times when mutual regulation of affect and motivation is occurring, self-regulation is also taking place.

What sense can a therapist or patient make of this diversity of views of motivation? We can compare analytic theoreticians to the fabled blind men examining different parts of an elephant. Each is accurate to some degree, but all are limited by the narrowness of their field of observation and prone to draw inaccurate conclusions. Or we can conclude that human experience is extremely complex, multidimensional, and highly context determined. From this perspective, when we consider an affect being sought at any experiential moment as central to an appreciation of motivation, we need to remain open to the complexity of desire, need, and values that might be involved. In a series of books, I have attempted to present and illustrate a view of motivation that is multidimensional and determined by self-determined need (self-regulation), the influence of external context (mutual regulation), and the interplay between them.

FIVE MOTIVATIONAL SYSTEMS

The type of theories that evoke confidence changes with time. We once viewed the brain, and by analogy, the psyche as a structure with parts that could be studied, dissected, and interpreted with objective reliability. Unconscious, preconscious, and conscious topographies and id, ego, and superego macrostructures grew out of that zeitgeist. In a postmodern world of relativity in which scientific predictions are at best probabilistic, more dynamic metaphors are required. The formation of systems balances stability (systems self-organize and self-stabilize) with change (dialectic tension is a constant force operating among components of systems and among systems). The persistence of internal and external tensions guarantees the reorganization of hierarchies throughout the life span. Some factors contribute to a remarkably stable sense of self-identity at different ages and under changing conditions such as the integrative power of the brain. Other factors contribute to the moment-to-moment ebb and flow of multiple senses of self, such as the ever-changing contexts of life.

From long study of the findings of infant research and empathic listening to patients of all ages, I have grouped the manifestations of human motivation into the functioning and regulation of five systems. Each system develops in response to definable needs that are present at birth and continue throughout life. Each need exerts an interactive force between caregiver and child, therapist and patient. Compatible needs and goals of both partners in a dyad open the way to an appropriate matching of responses by one to an accurate recognition of the needs and desires of the other, thereby promoting the development of each and of the dyadic relationship. Divergent needs and goals promote mismatches and competing interests and result in aversiveness. The patterning of these matches and mismatches establishes expectations that shape the development of future relationships and the unfolding of motivational expression within them.

Nutrient intake, elimination of wastes, breathing, tactile and proprioceptive activity, warmth, sleep, and general health are physiological requirements that serve to initiate patterns of response. The patterns go smoothly when psychic regulation of bodily function interdigitates effectively with provisions by the human and physical environment. For each physiological requirement, the mental state combines affects and bodily sensations. The emotions range from the quiet pleasures of soft touch, to an infant's whimpering before sleep, to the desperation of not being able to breathe in an asthma attack. The emotional realm of the physiological motivational system has unique subterranean connections to other systems. The patterns of bodily experience can be taken over by other realms, as Freud noted in connecting the symbolism involved in the stubbornness of the child resisting toilet training to the tightness of the miser. Likewise, suppressed affects, as in attachment relationships, may gain expression in bodily forms such as eating disorders, muscular tenseness, or insomnia.

The development of an attachment motivational system has been studied in conjunction with the need for a sense of safety, self-cohesion, and worth; for competence in communication with self and others; and for a feeling of belonging to family, society, and culture. At a moment of danger or loss, infants seek safety by developing a secure base from the responsiveness of a caregiver to their signals of distress. Caregivers' success in relieving distress enables their children to develop both a secure attachment and an increasing capacity for self-reliance balanced with reliance on others. The success of the early self- and mutual regulatory lived moments between child and caregiver establish expectations of similar competence in meeting the challenges of future attachment experiences.

Caregivers who are too caught up in their own troubled preoccupations leave their insecurely attached children to evolve strategies that involve both anxious seeking and wary reluctance to be soothed into safety. The push–pull form of attachment these children follow contributes to the likelihood that as adults they will remain preoccupied with the difficulty they have had in achieving intimacy.

Caregivers who are withdrawn, cold, discontented, and often angry foster a strategy of avoidance in their children. To prevent the rejection they anticipate, these children avoid both directly seeking attachment and exposing their distress. This strategy allows them to establish an equilibrium that permits them to coexist in the general orbit of the caregiver, gaining what safety they can, but not without considerable internal affective and autonomic nervous system stress. As adults, they tend to dismiss the impact of events and their feelings. They avoid intimate contact and tend to be self-reliant while craving support and attention.

Caregivers whose responses lie outside the range of what is tolerable for their children, who frighten or overexcite or excessively shame them, or who behave in freakish unpredictable ways, leave their children unable to form any coherent strategy that preserves a sense of safety. These children experience moments of disorganization, detachment, and even dissociation. As adults, they experience considerable difficulty recognizing and reflecting on their own mental states and regulating their emotions, especially in response to stress.

What are the affects sought when attachment motives predominate? Infants and adults seek connection to others not only for safety, but also for affection, intimacy, and self-worth. A smile shown and a smile returned activates affection. A hand extended when a hand is desired conveys the intimacy of knowing the other. An accomplishment, however small, when responded to with encouragement and appreciation, builds self-worth. An acknowledgment of the desirability of your company by someone you greatly respect augments your self-respect. A strongly shared feeling, preference, or opinion conveys the sense of being able to form an intimate connection with another person. During treatment, acknowledging accomplishments with others or with the therapist (mirroring) offers encouragement to patients in their struggles to improve their attachments and increases the patient–therapist bond.

Along with the needs and desires of children for secure attachments to individual caregivers, children have strong needs and desires for affiliation with groups. Human life begins in a familial "community," however small (even a single mother and her baby), that is embedded in a larger group and culture. Within an ordinary family, an infant can gain a sense of her participation in a cooperative individual relationship, and in a group affiliation, from the manner in which the parents handle the exigencies of their own lives and hers. At inevitable times of stress, such as an infant or toddler's aversiveness, or external or intramarital events, can they work together sensitively? Or does one or both parents, or other influential people in the child's life, try to coopt the child into an alliance with their sorrows, angers, or fears? Finally, have the parents allowed their own stress level to reach the point where they are unable to provide a coherent way to deal with each other, the external world, and especially the child's needs, leaving the child with no confidence that he can be safe in any affiliate experience (school, club, team)?

In a quest for the affect being experienced and the affect being sought, we recognize the ubiquity of relational or attachment linkages. Paradoxically, however, much of life is spent dealing with nonhuman objects and sorting out issues and problems in one's own mind. Winnicott addressed this paradox in reference to a child at play with toys as developing the capacity to be alone in the presence of the other. Winnicott described how young children use their imagination and "transitional objects" such as blankets to retain or create a sense of a supportive other in her absence. We could think of this capacity as being able, when apart from immediate human contact, to enjoy solitude while playing, exploring, or asserting influence on the nonpersonal world. To be able to be comfortable when alone is a valuable capacity, but to be at play with toys, doing homework, or working at an adult task are all inspired by a powerful assortment of sought-after affects: interest, efficacy, and competence. In some individuals, these affects may not be sufficient to offset the discomfort evoked by being alone. Then assertive exploration may be inhibited without the actual presence of a supportive person.

The motivational system underlying these activities is based on the need for exploration and the assertion of preferences. The affect of interest activates the system. We can recognize this system when an infant alerts and scans the surroundings, fixing her attention on a preferred "object" like the human face, an earring, or a favorite toy. We use this system when we "distract" a fussy infant by catching his interest with a rattle and noting the instantaneous switching off of the aversive system and turning on of the exploratory system. Once activated, that is, once turned on by interest, children continue to explore an area of preference, motivated to activate a sense of efficacy and competence and an overall sense of mastery. Efficacy, competence, and mastery sound sobering as affects to be sought, but the vitalizing affective element in the exploratory system arises from involvement in play. The feelings aroused when involved in play may be fun, interest stirred by novelty, the satisfaction of improvisation and problem solving, and the excitement of competition. Children work hard at their play, whether alone or especially with peers, and they want to get good at it once it has tweaked their interest. Adolescents will forgo sleep to finish a book, work out a problem, or compete in a computer game. Adults who can imbue their work with play, who maintain a world of imagination, and who balance occupation with recreation achieve considerable fulfillment.

Aversive motivation presents an exception to the principle of seeking a positive affect as a guide to a person's dominant motivation. Discerning an affect being experienced in a troubling event that a patient is describing straightforwardly may reveal anger, fear, dread, distress, envy, sadness, depression, boredom, disappointment, shame, humiliation, embarrassment, contempt, confusion, disorientation, or dissociation. In general we don't find that patients seek these negative affects. A person may choose to go to a scary movie, but the goal is to experience fear in a controlled situation with a known ending rather than to set off a fear state. As after a disturbing dream, the awakening dreamer can seek comfort from asserting that it was only a dream, the moviegoer can leave the theater saying it was only a story. The excitement and pleasure of mastery may be more important than the fear itself. However, patients so regularly get themselves into situations outside and inside the treatment that trigger fear or anger or envy or shame or depression that negative affect states would appear to be their perverse goal, a motivation they are compelled to repeat.

I construe the tragic repetition differently. When attachment experiences in infancy have established patterns of insecure connections or when traumatic events at any time in life have adversely affected self-regulation, expectations are established that skew the patient's perceptual bias toward failed experiences of self with other. The likelihood is greater that a relationship or an event will be experienced with fear rather than safety, with envy or shame rather than pride, with anger rather than acceptance and calm. Many subsequent good experiences must occur to convince a downbeat person to perceive a bright future, and only a few disappointments are sufficient to lose that conviction. Of course the powerful determinants of these skewing expectations are unconscious, as are the troubled self-with-other maps or schemas on which the expected repetition is based. Intimacy or its anticipation may trigger the expectation of inevitable disappointment, automatically triggering aversive affects linked to scenarios of prior experience. Accordingly, bringing the manifestations of these biases and their experiential triggers into awareness is a central goal of therapeutic exploration.

The unpleasantness of fear, envy, shame, and sadness suggests that the goal of parenting or treatment would be to work for their reduction or removal. So it is in the neonate and in early infancy. Caregivers who recognize their infant's signs of crying, hunger, distress, fear, and anger as signals for relief establish themselves as a secure base. Caregivers' optimal responses combine needed actions with an appropriate emotional response. Emotionally, caregivers must recognize the distress and share the feeling to a degree, but not be overwhelmed by it. Sharing the child's emotion during a distress state while maintaining a perspective that the child will get over it helps infants to gain confidence that their aversive affects can be regulated and contained.

In the second year, the motivational needs of the aversive system shift from a primary focus on relieving the sources of negative affect to helping toddlers utilize their negative affective experiences to find their own adaptive solutions. An important accomplishment of the toddler period is that of learning how to regulate anger and opposition so as to be effective in controversy, without sacrificing the ability to restore relations with an adversary or the capacity to restore one's own calm. Envy and shame can become a spur to achievement and pride, and fear can become a much-needed component of the ability to assess danger and institute a strategic withdrawal or other defensive measures. During treatment, patients often need to be helped to recognize and utilize anger and fear. Assertiveness backed up by anger is needed to be effective in controversy and to experience a sense of power. Fear and an assessment of risk are needed to recognize and cope with danger.

The affect being sought through sensuality is pleasure, the pleasure of affection and the delight of an arousing or a soothing sensation. The affect being sought via sexuality is the excitement of orgasm and postorgasm relaxation. Sexual excitement is more focused, while sensuality is more protean. The pleasure of sensuality may be evoked by various body experiences and by the beauty of nature, music, and artistic form. Ideally, sexual partners are able to cocreate and integrate the affectionate pleasure–excitement experiences of sensuality and orgastic pursuit. Often people may misconstrue a sensual goal, for example, if a desire for gentle affection is taken for a sexual invitation or provocation. Another type of misconception has led to significant revision of the view we hold of the sensual–sexual motivational system. This misconception lay in treating social distinctions of gender, male and female, and of practices, straight or gay, as fixed categories. This pseudo-biological, largely moralistic stance has given way to a broadly relativistic view. The influence of feminist theorists, such as Benjamin, Chodorow, and Harris, has contributed to the openness of many analysts to reconsider time-honored "certainties." Empathic listening without bias reveals that a male (female), no matter how masculine (feminine) in a traditional social sense, will employ strategies and seek affective experiences that are traditionally female (male). The gender identities of both men and women are comparably multidimensional and responsive in variable ways to the requirements of different contexts. This flexibility in pursuit of sensual pleasure and sexual excitement is observable in relational, romantic, and lovemaking practices, in what is sought in a partner, and particularly in fantasies and dreams.

What benefits can a therapist derive from conceptualizing motivational systems? In chapter 2, I described the significance of systematically sensing into the mind of the patient. The five motivational systems provide a map to guide and orient therapists as to the type of desires, stresses, conflicts, and values that accrue around each fundamental need. All too often, therapists guided by a less comprehensive theoretical schema will privilege one set of desires without being open to a broader range of what they might consider to be a patient's current, immediately dominant theme. Depending on their theory and view of development, therapists have focused their listening and interpreting on sexuality, attachment, or aggression. Elements of each of these omnipresent human motives can be teased out of most clinical renderings but may not be central to the narrative the patient is relating. If an analyst insists on addressing a patient's anger at him when a patient wants to talk about his deep concern about weight or her feeling of panic about a work assignment, an empathic failure is inevitable, with a disruption likely to follow. Ironically, the analyst could then come to believe he was "right," and the patient's resistance to accept the accuracy of the interpretation is why the patient is now angry with him. The situation in the therapy would be analogous to a mother who mistook her infant's hunger cry or desire to explore and play as an indication that the baby was angry with her. I believe that the more inclusive and broadly based map provided by motivational systems theory increases the likelihood that the therapist will be in touch with the immediate dominant theme of the patient. The affects of clinical moments are the "golden threads" that guide a therapist's skill in discerning what might be the dominant motivational system involved.

This benefit is amplified by consideration of the affects being sought, not only those achieved in the moment, as discussed earlier in this chapter. Therapists often have more difficulty discovering the affect sought than the affect experienced. Patients, too, may lose track of the affect sought, especially when the actions under consideration are long-term, repetitive patterns. Compulsive habits such as hair twirling, repetitive patterns such as bulimia or bullying, and, particularly, addictive patterns such as gambling, substance abuse, or certain sexual practices are often performed as if they have no connection to a recognizable affective goal that makes sense to the doer; thus they have frequently been waste-basketed as masochistic.

Motivational systems theory offers two frames of reference useful to patients and therapists alike in unlocking the mystery of what they are seeking through detached repetitive patterns. One frame of reference is that each system involves particular forms and requirements of regulation of affective intensity. Affective regulation applies to each specific form of bodily need, the distancing and intimacy of attachment, the ability to focus and concentrate on tasks of play and work, the management of controversy and danger, and the ups and downs of stimulation in sensuality and sexuality. A second frame of reference is that each system involves affective goals or affect-laden values. Affective goals and values involve body sensations such as hunger and thirst, relief and satiety; affection, intimacy, and loyalty; heightened interest, playfulness, efficacy, competence, and confidence; power, influence, control, vengeance, safety, and sanctuary; soothing, vitalizing, potency, surrender, orgasm, and relaxation. Thus, questioning what affect is being sought by a difficult-to-explain behavior or symptom requires opening an inquiry to what goal from the patient's point of view he is seeking and what affect is associated with that goal.

Damon grew up in a wealthy, prominent, but dysfunctional family. He mentioned that he wanted to avoid his mother since his own son had casually let her know that he didn't get the courses he wanted at college. His mother had gone on a tear about the school being no good. Damon added that this reaction came on top of another rant regarding her hate of the president. Damon had shown her a magazine article documenting the president's errors, and now she was harassing him to get the article for her. I noted that, like his son, he had set off her easily inflamed outrage and the pummeling of him that followed. He agreed, saying that he hated her exaggeration, her wild swings of mood and opinion. I suggested that unlike his son, he knew from many past experiences what would happen. I took him back to a scene we had puzzled over many times. Damon managed the family finances, and at a time when his mother was moving from one house to another in rapid states of dissatisfaction, stretching her finances, he took her to see a magnificent home he had discovered that was far above even her considerable resources. As he might have expected, she immediately wanted it, and much contention followed until she finally gave up her preoccupation with it. I asked him to try to put himself into his state of mind at the time. He remembered that each of his siblings had been creating quite a stir and that his mother was dismissive and contemptuous of him as a grubby businessman, whereas she and they were creative artists. I asked how he thought she saw him when he showed her the house. "Oh" he said, "she thought I was a genius, that I could really appreciate beauty." I suggested then that they could share a high and that he had felt the elation of her appreciation. He added, "Yes for the moment, and then, as always, came the aftermath." With the magazine article, I suggested, he could also give her what she wanted; he could be the special one to feed her excitement of outrage and again have the moment of feeling the intensity of a special bond.

The example of Damon describes puzzling, repeated, problematic actions that had an out-of-awareness goal of ensuring an attachment motivation to feel appreciated and special (mirrored). I can refer also to the earlier presented case of Larry, whose elation over his gambling losses could only be understood from his point of view, that is, in conjunction with his physiological motivation for elimination relief. Alice Scott was a talented young woman with many borderline symptoms and severe depressive episodes. She had been emotionally and physically abused as a child. Whenever stress arose, she would either be blisteringly antagonistic or would withdraw for days. If these aversive strategies failed to reduce her tension, she would resort to delicate cutting with a razor. During a session in which she was becoming increasingly tense and distressed, I became alarmed as the ending approached. From prior episodes I feared that she would leave and begin cutting. To my question, she acknowledged that this was just what she was planning and could hardly stay in her chair. I began to anticipate visually a really bad episode in which she would cut not only her wrists, but also her neck, as she had done before when the wrist cutting didn't suffice. Spontaneously, without forethought, I said, "Do it now." "What?" she said. "Do it now; you have a razor in your hand, do it now with me here." Her fingers closed around the imagined razor, and she carefully began to make "cuts" in her wrist, measuring the depth, and then recutting to get greater depth. She was completely self-occupied in a dissociative trance. Finally, she said, "Oh there it's bleeding now," and it was as if we could both see the blood welling up and dripping down. A few seconds later, she heaved a great sigh of relief, looked directly up at me, and said, "I feel OK now. I'm ready to leave." The affect being experienced was a complete absorption in pain and its control, the affect being sought was relief, a release from unbearable tension by self-inflicted control of pain.

Unlike Alice, who regulated the effect of her physical abuse by utilizing strategies of the aversive motivational system, Mary Jane used pain to regulate the trauma of sexual abuse perpetuated by a trusted friend of her family. Her family denied her accusations, blaming her for lying and being a troublemaker. She had been promiscuous as an adolescent but felt that neither her brief involvements with men nor the sexual experiences gave her satisfaction. She searched through the Internet until she found the "perfect" partner. To help me understand (although she doubted that I would), she brought me a picture of a woman with needles in her breasts and genitalia. Her partner had acquired all the needed apparatus and the skills to use it. As with Alice Scott, pain was involved and required the most delicate control. For Mary Jane, however, the pain was part of a dyadic regulation, a demonstration of commonality of purpose and working together. The state of arousal achieved through a mix of pain and sensual sensation led finally to an orgastic sexual experience with postcoital relief. The experience being sought was Mary Jane's fantasy of ideal love conveyed through the perfect attunement of pain and erotic intensification.

In this chapter, I indicated the significance of a therapist's focus on emotions to gain entry into a patient's state of mind. I have emphasized the place of tracking the emotions that had been experienced during an event and the emotions that are involved in a patient's intentions. In the next chapter I will shift to a focus on speech. I will describe guidelines that promote bringing into focus the elements of a patient's verbal rendering of experience that facilitate or obscure a therapist's attempt to share the patient's experience and intentions.

CHAPTER 4

"THE MESSAGE CONTAINS THE MESSAGE"

OPENING COMMUNICATION TO ITS FULLEST REVELATION

THE APPROACH I EMPHASIZE IN THIS CHAPTER, "the message contains the message," sounds more like a maxim than a guideline for psychotherapists. My intention in proposing it is to reorient the manner in which therapists attend to the flow of a patient's communication. I recommend listening to each patient's narrative, his or her unique rendering of an event or description and explanation of a symptom for what is stated as well as what is implied. Shifting from a skeptical stance of a detective listening for what is hidden, therapists attending to what is in or is close to awareness affirms for patients the value of their spontaneous associations, of their version of the story of their life as they bring it into their awareness. Listening in this way, therapists avoid communicating to a patient that the patient's message is really an attempt to divert both therapist and self from something else. Implied in such a listening stance is that what is not presented is necessarily of more therapeutic importance than what is presented. Guided by "the message contains the message," therapists see and hear the total delivered communication from the patient: verbal, gestural, and facial. They attempt to familiarize themselves with their patients' intentions as the patient consciously wishes them to be known. When listened to in this way, patients feel safer to express themselves more freely and feel an enhanced esteem that allows them to explore and reflect in greater depth. In this way, patients are encouraged to make previously hidden or unconscious motives and messages more accessible to awareness.

Communication involves multiple points of selection. Our familiar invitation to a patient to say what comes into his mind implies that selections of psychological contents are made in or near conscious awareness. Using speech as an example (and remembering that speech is but one form of communication), we can recognize the various levels of selection that contribute to what a patient ends up telling a therapist. First is a selection operating at the body–brain level that involves adjusting the signal intensity of internal and external perceptions. The brain is consistently receiving information from a multitude of perceptual pathways. Consequently, selection at the body–brain level is absolutely necessary because so many stimulus inputs are present at all times that adaptive relevance must be preserved. All of this process is outside of and unavailable to conscious awareness. At a second level, the conscious product of the body–brain processing of bioperceptual information, what we refer to as cognition and emotion, gives substance and form to our inner speech, our inner monologue–dialogue, and our dreams. Inner speech, which may be words, images, and sensations, is a monologue in that it is from oneself to oneself but also a dialogue in that the shadow of another as audience is always implicit—sometimes explicit. Although inner speech is most commonly verbal employing a loose syntax, dreams, the product of sleep mentation, are primarily imagistic. Because inner speech and dream imagery tend to be rapid, the transition to dialogic discourse requires slowing down and grammatical revision as well as an unconscious and conscious strategic selection of what to reveal and what to hold back. The selection process is made both as a form of self-regulation, largely at the prespeech level, and mutual regulation, largely at the level of dialogic speech. Each message that contains the message combines the influence of prior forms of self- and mutual regulation with a current version selectively and uniquely cocreated that emerges in response to the challenge of the specific clinical moment.

For the therapist, unconscious and conscious selection occurs at the same diverse levels, and spoken communication is also chosen on the basis of unique self-generated criteria and with the receptivity of the patient as a criterion. Therapists have the additional task of selecting their principal focus of attention from among all the possible elements communicated by the patient. Successful inferences about the meaning of experiences derive from those elements of the patient's communication to which therapists attach primary significance. Analytic theory began with the premise that behind the immediate content of a communication lay a hidden message. Free association, that is, the patient faithfully reporting every thought as it came to mind, had the aim of opening censored content to observation. The theory held that once a patient's communication was free of censorship, the analyst could look behind the reported associations to infer the hidden message. Freud used the metaphor of an archaeological search in which archaeologists dig down through layer after layer to find the "truth" about earlier events. Similarly, analysts regarded themselves as digging down through layers of defenses, current experiences, and revisions of past events to find the truth about childhood traumas or fantasies based on drive distortions.

A positivist maxim is that "the truth shall set you free." This led to the logical premise that, if patients beset with psychoneurotic symptoms would learn about the unresolved childhood conflicts that were presumed to be the source of their symptoms, they could use their insight and adult logic to make a nonsymptomatic adaptation to life problems. In its fundamental assertion that discovery and understanding lead to psychic transformation, this remarkable hypothesis of Freud remains a guiding principle in all analytic-based therapies. The focus on penetrating through (by analysis of them) defenses to hidden contents remains the approach of many analytic therapists, but others focus more on the immediate experience of their patients with them (the here and now of "us") to gain crucial information. They give precedence to recognizing and interpreting the relational interaction that is and has developed in the dyad.

My focus includes both attending to the relational interaction and broadening the range of focus beyond it because I believe patients include far more in the message as delivered than a dyadic communication. The principal difference that has led me to abandon the archaeological metaphor as my guide is my belief that to search for what is behind the message as delivered or what is hidden by it denigrates its communicative value. To find the needle in the haystack treats the hay as only an impediment. My approach is to seek all the meaning a patient and I can extract from the messages we are sending each other. This approach allows therapists to be equally attentive to all sides of the patient's communication. After all, each message contains mixed elements of what a person consciously wants the listener to know, what a person unconsciously wants the listener to know (they often are not the same), what a person consciously doesn't want the listener to know, and what a person unconsciously wants to hide from the listener (including himself) or to deceive him about. By conceptualizing communication in this way, that "the message contains the message," both the hay and the needle are explored and yield equally important information about the patient and the dyadic relationship.

The therapist's listening priorities that derive from "the message contains the message" begin with what a patient can acknowledge that she wants to be telling. The explicit communication may involve a feeling, an event, a dream, a complaint, a request. It may be in the form of an organized story, fragments of loose associations, chatty time fillers, long silences, emotional storms, or contemplative reflective observations about self or others. Therapists' listening priority extends beyond being an attentive faithful recorder of the delivered message to attempt to track a theme unfolding as the session or sessions progress. Developing an intuitive sensing of a theme or motivational story about self with others involves integrating the explicit message of consciously intended communication with an implicit message of unconsciously intended communication.

An expensively dressed, successful professional woman wore pantyhose with rips and snags as a message to her therapist of the feeling of neglect from childhood she still experienced every day. A man who prided himself on his affability and positive orientation to his treatment would start to shake his foot in annoyance if he felt his therapist did not respond as quickly as he wished. A man who regarded himself as timid would raise his eyebrows in contempt and disdain as he described his troubled relations with superiors. Gestures, facial expression, vocal tone, eye contact or aversion, grooming, clothing, posture, perspiration, body tension, odor, and gait are all omnipresent elements of implicit communication that are being absorbed directly or subliminally by an attentive therapist. A therapist may recognize the implicit message as an augmentation of the explicit message or as a contradiction to it. His awareness of either explicit or implicit communication may, at times, emerge more from focusing on his own emotional responses than from observation of the patient.

Arthur Harris was a patient whose adventurous young adult years gave him interesting experiences to relate. A major complaint was that although he easily attracted women, before long their interest in him faded and the affairs petered out. In the middle phase of his analysis, I could follow his associations from within his perspective for the first 10 or 15 minutes of the session, during which he would report significant events or dreams. Then my attention would drift off. My attempts to explain my flagging responsiveness to his explicit or implicit message were unproductive. When I turned to introspection, I failed to relate it to any conflictual response on my part to the content of his associations or to him personally. During one session, I connected the drifting of my attention to an experience I remembered having when I sat with my children watching a TV show in which I had only a distant interest. I would attend to the TV show enough to talk about it with them, but otherwise, I would think my own thoughts. Within a few moments, Arthur mentioned (as he had previously) that when he came home after work he turned the TV on, made dinner, and let the evening drift away without getting to work on his long overdue tax-refund claim. Cued by my association, I asked him about his reference to turning on the TV. He described a state of mind in which he would begin to listen to the news, and then the TV would become a general background blur that he would tune in and out of awareness. His recent girlfriend had complained about it for a while but then said nothing more.

Once this drifting state of mind came into focus for us, we were able to relate it to his use of alcohol and marijuana—not to enhance his experience (as he had claimed), but to produce this sense of being with another in a state of remoteness and drift. Stimulated by dream images of furniture placement in his childhood apartment, he began to recall a seemingly innocuous scene, which served as a nodal point (a model scene, see chapter 7) for our joint effort to reconstruct significant family relationships and their effect on him. In this scene, he was sprawled out on the floor with the TV on in front of him. His mother was sitting behind him, on the other side of the room, knitting or reading. His father had gone to work, leaving him, as he saw it, to keep his lonely, depressed mother company. In desultory fashion, he watched TV while flipping a rope, imagined to be a cowboy's lariat, over a chair. There was no conversation between him and his mother; the only sounds came from the TV. His attention was dominated by anger-filled fantasies of heroic battles. A mood of depressed remoteness, irritability, and mutual withholding characterized the exchange. An appreciation of this scene provided welcome entry into the reenactment that we had cocreated in such a puzzling fashion. We had unconsciously drifted into the roles of two people similar to his mother and him passing time in a desultory state while the TV (his droning speech) played in the background. The message indeed contained the message, but, to decode it, I had to go beyond what I could recognize from either his explicit or implicit communication. In retrospect, I believe that earlier, more perceptive appreciation of his vocal tones, body posture, and breathing might have provided clues to the message he was unconsciously communicating. In any event, I began to discover the message contained in (not hidden by) the message as delivered via his dream images and our cocreated model scene.

Freud's archaeological metaphor does apply to some extremely obscure symptoms. These symptoms contain the message as an artifact of traumatic occurrences in the individual's past life. These experiences remain as physiological revenants that preceded or escaped symbolic representation so that the symptom stands alone as both message and container. An example comes from the treatment of Mrs. G.

Mrs. G's therapy centered on her phobic symptoms, her depression, and her hypersensitivity to anxiety. She described a symptom that was unique in my experience. Her mouth would be held open as if to yawn but, unlike a yawn, she would not inspire air. Instead, she would try to get her mouth to close. We spoke of this as a yawn for lack of a better designation and related it to a response to mounting anxiety. Yet this coupling with anxiety struck me as unsatisfactory because I couldn't determine why this particular response should occur rather than any of her other responses to anxiety.

Mrs. G became generally able to associate to and master anxiety. Her "yawn" disappeared or, more accurately, did not occur (neither of us being aware of its absence). Then, during the final months of her lengthy therapy, Mrs. G was telling me an anecdote about her new baby and her five-year-old daughter. She seemed rather comfortable, and I was listening with my attention easily placed within her state of mind. She described feeding the baby a bottle, with her daughter looking on and asking if she could help. Somewhat reluctantly, Mrs. G answered "yes" and gave her the baby and the bottle. After turning away for a moment, she looked back to see the baby in some distress because the five-year-old feeder had let the bottle press too deeply into the baby's mouth. Mrs. G proceeded to describe her reason for bringing up this anecdote. Initially she had been ready to react with a panicky yell. She was pleased that she had been able to get control of herself and simply help her daughter reposition the bottle properly. As she talked, I basked somewhat in her pride of mastery over her inclination to panic and her implied appreciation of me as the parent–therapist who had helped her to do so. Involuntarily, without conscious thought, I found myself opening my mouth and feeling the sensation of a nipple thrust into it too far to suck in or push out. I repeated to her this aspect of her description before asking her about my conjecture that her so-called yawning symptom was a somatic memory of a nipple thrust too far into *her* mouth. Before I could verbalize my question, she reproduced the symptom for the first time in several years.

The construction we made was based on a great deal of information about her early life. A premature baby, she had spent two months in an incubator before coming home. This gap probably interfered with the attachment between mother and infant, which was also attenuated by the mother's general anxiety and preoccupation with her own mother's chronic physical illness. We postulated that her mother, pulled by this concern, had at times turned over aspects of Mrs. G's care to Mrs. G's older sister. Whatever difficulties had occurred, especially mechanical ones of a too-intrusive nipple, may have been aggravated by the mouth sensitivity of this premature child, plus a degree of weakness in thrusting the bottle away. What was most fascinating to me was that dream material related to this experience appeared only after the exploratory work. Work with this material led to associative links to conflicts over impingement. Yet dreams prior to this construction, viewed retrospectively, did not reveal that the bodily registry had received a symbolic representation, as far as I could discern. The symptom alone had contained the message.

In more usual therapeutic exchanges, patients fill the receptive openness of the session with an issue or issues they believe will help them gain a desired goal. In the opening moments of a session, sometimes in a seemingly casual aside, as in the clinical example to follow, patients often convey an implicit message. The opening message and the entire dialogue that ensues between patient and therapist can be looked on as a text that can be scanned to bring forward overt or embedded themes that organize the message as a whole. The text that allows therapists to illuminate and track themes as they wax and wane is not limited to the message as delivered by the patient but involves the totality of the interchange and the therapist's ongoing introspection, inference making, and interventions. The text is not simply a patient's message combined with a therapist's message: she said plus I said plus she said. The text of an ongoing exploratory therapy is shaped by the relatedness the pair has achieved as evidenced by the conversational and conceptual space they offer each other and the hints and cues they communicate.

CLINICAL EXAMPLE

Sylvia is a married woman with one child. Because of a collagen disease requiring steroids, she has had to give up her profession. This change in her life aggravated her tendency to be somewhat reclusive and to be dismissive of aversive feelings. Behind her avoidant pattern lay traumatizing problems with both parents, which had been intensified by her divided loyalties after their divorce.

Sylvia announces the theme of the hour in her opening comment about missing her daughter on her first day of school. Here the message is packaged in the social convention of an entry comment not meant explicitly to be the business of the session. I have found that such "social" comments often are highly pertinent, like an opening chord in a musical composition before the formal theme is announced. Naturally, the motif significance of "missing" can only be appreciated later in the hour when missing reappears in several different contexts. Also noteworthy is the difference between the opening mention where Sylvia talks explicitly about missing her daughter, and the later references, where missing must be inferred implicitly as Sylvia disconnects herself from the emotional experience.

Tracking a transcript of a therapy session differs from tracking an authored text. A text authored by a single person tends to present themes in a relatively linear fashion for better comprehension. The therapeutic transcript of necessity introduces strong nonlinear elements in that a therapist's spoken or unspoken interventions introduce a constant influence, leading themes emanating from the patient to wax or wane. The extent of the influence at any moment is unpredictable in that small encouragements may have considerable effect at one moment and none at another, and small failures to comprehend may pass unnoticed, be a minor distraction, or be a major dysjunction. While Sylvia and her therapist are each contributing to the flow of the theme about missing and the subtheme of coldness and anger, together they cocreate an atmosphere that transcends the immediate exchanges. The message of the session contains the unfolding of messages expressing both missing and coldness themes and a created ambiance of generally moving along together, trying to follow each other's leads and include each other's point of view.

PATIENT: First day of school—D (seven-year-old daughter) is very excited—I'm going to miss her but that's OK. She is happy to be back with her friends.

THERAPIST: So, she got off OK this morning.

PATIENT: Yeah, everything went fine—she was so happy.
THERAPIST: That's good.

PATIENT: This weekend was weird. I got my steroids on Friday and I was just off this weekend—hyper as hell and then I crashed suddenly on Sunday and I got down and hyper and mean.
THERAPIST: Tell me about that—what happened?

PATIENT: I just wasn't very nice.
THERAPIST: To M (husband)?

PATIENT: And D sometimes—I just got frustrated.
THERAPIST: Was there anything especially upsetting?

PATIENT: No, just how I felt.
THERAPIST: Do you usually have that kind of reaction to the steroids?

PATIENT: Not usually that bad—but I always can tell when I've had the shot. But we did have couples counseling last night, which wasn't a good idea.
THERAPIST: Why is that?

PATIENT: Well, I really hurt his feelings—poor guy.
THERAPIST: Well, tell me.

PATIENT: Well, we talked about the phone—he has a habit of calling me up in the middle of the day from work and putting me on hold for hours—so I just hang up.
THERAPIST: So you get pretty pissed off about being forgotten? [The analyst illuminates the contained message by identifying the affect involved in hanging up—being pissed off—and the source—being forgotten.]

PATIENT: Yeah. Also *I* don't want to call *him*. When he's gone, he's gone—but when he's home, he's home.
THERAPIST: Can you tell me about those feelings?

PATIENT: Well, when he's at work doing his own thing, I feel disconnected—he thinks that we are each just doing our own thing but are still connected. When people aren't there, I put them in a funny place in my brain.
THERAPIST: What's that funny place like?

PATIENT: I don't know—they are gone—you don't see them or think about them, so I don't want to call them.
THERAPIST: So I guess the phone calls disturb your effort to keep them in that funny place.

PATIENT: Right!
THERAPIST: So what happens to your feelings for him during these phone calls?

PATIENT: Well, it depends—but he usually ends up putting me on hold.
THERAPIST: So what is that feeling?

PATIENT: Well, disturbed—by being put on hold. It's similar to *saying goodbye* to my family—it used to be different, but now I just put them in that place and they are gone.
THERAPIST: So at some point it was very hard until you developed this place?

PATIENT: Yeah, the first few years.
THERAPIST: And you really *missed* them during this period? [Through the reference to saying good-bye, Sylvia returns to the theme of missing that the therapist identifies precisely.]

PATIENT: Yeah, a little is okay—I just overdo it.
THERAPIST: And how do you overdo it?

PATIENT: You're there but not there, so instead of integrating it into my life it upsets the balance. [Pause] [During this pause, the therapist had to consider whether Sylvia was moving the therapist's absence into the foreground in her shift to the

personal pronoun "you" or whether the foreground is occupied by the pressure of her memory of missing her family of origin.]
THERAPIST: It sounds like you feel that you have gotten too upset by this in the past—by the family separations. [Going back and forth between parents and then leaving Europe where her family lives and she grew up.]

PATIENT: Maybe . . . I don't know. I don't want to not function, so I keep things very separate—I think I'm a little overorganized.
THERAPIST: When you say that you keep things separate, do you mean the practical and the emotions? [In her response, Sylvia moves away from the past to return to the present with her current family, and the therapist shifts with her.]

PATIENT: When my family is there I interact with them, when they are not I don't.
THERAPIST: So they go into a sort of cold storage? [The therapist is trying to demonstrate that the message includes an understated affective thread first by his phrasing of "too upset" and "practical and the emotions" and then by the evocative metaphor of "cold storage."]

PATIENT: Yeah, M got very upset about this.
THERAPIST: What was it that you said?

PATIENT: Well, that I did not want him to call me during the day.
THERAPIST: Did he understand any of what we are talking about today?

PATIENT: No, but do you get it? [Sylvia now calls on the therapist directly to do more than ask exploratory questions. She directly requests that he convey his understanding of her explicit and implicit message.]
THERAPIST: Well, I think so. It seems like the upset that you experienced during separations has led you to develop this place—this cold storage where you keep people and that this place allows you to function—essentially go about your business

without feeling the absences so acutely. And it seems your ability to keep M in this place is disturbed by these phone calls, which in themselves are frustrating because he ends up putting you on hold while he attends to business. The end result leaves you feeling that it would almost be better not to talk to him during the day and just wait till he's home because that is the way you use to cope with separations. Does that seem right so far? [Sensing that he is giving Sylvia a somewhat complex explanation, the therapist pauses before going further to give her a chance to agree or modify.]

PATIENT: Yeah. That seems right.
THERAPIST: It also seems that there is this feeling that your ability to put people in this place—"out of sight, out of mind"—makes you wonder if you're a bit coldhearted. [Reassured that Sylvia believes they have achieved an adequate mutual understanding, the therapist invites Sylvia to reflect on the cost to her of obliterating the image of people she cares about—being coldhearted—a concern she had expressed in the beginning of the session as being mean and hurtful to M.]

PATIENT: Yeah, I guess it's part of why I don't call people as much—because it upsets things.
THERAPIST: It upsets keeping them in this place [pause], and I would imagine it makes it tough to take them back in after the phone call.

PATIENT: No, I'm pretty good at it actually [crying]. [At this point, the message contained in the message of Sylvia's tears is unrevealed. Does she feel moved by the sadness of separation? Does she feel hurt by an implied criticism of her as coldhearted? Is she sad because of the loneliness of her withdrawal?]
[Pause]
THERAPIST: Tell me, do you think you might have done the same thing with your father when you missed him? [With the disconnect that follows Sylvia's crying, the therapist might have attempted to explore the meaning of her tears. Instead, he uses

his association to attempt to reopen the issue of missing by selecting her father, whom she lost twice, first through her parents' divorce and second by moving from Europe.]

PATIENT: Probably—I don't know.
THERAPIST: Well that would make some sense—it does sound like a technique that was born of some real emotional pain. [Sensing the need signaled by Sylvia's intellectual "probably—I don't know" to shift back and respond to Sylvia's emotion, the therapist reconnects by acknowledging the source of her "funny place" as "real emotional pain."]

PATIENT: Yeah—so how do I get rid of it?
THERAPIST: So it is something you want to get rid of?

PATIENT: Yeah I think so.
THERAPIST: Because of the way it makes you feel about yourself?

PATIENT: That and because I would like to keep better contact with people, and people are probably hurt by it.
THERAPIST: Have people said things to you about it?

PATIENT: Well, my oldest sister wants me to call even when things are not going on.
THERAPIST: But that would mean keeping her out of this place.

PATIENT: Right. Not that I don't want to—I just find it difficult. [A longer pause]
[Sylvia had asked directly for helpful advice—"how do I get rid of it?—and the therapist had parried her request. He might have recognized and possibly opened for discussion this interplay in which he answered one question and dodged another. Instead, he took up an earlier theme that had been left incomplete.]
THERAPIST: So you felt pretty bad about hurting M's feelings last night? [An attempt to fill out the reference to hurting her husband's feelings from earlier in the session.]

PATIENT: Yeah, because he was so upset that he couldn't sleep.
THERAPIST: How did you think he was hearing what you said to him?

PATIENT: That I don't care about him. [Pause] How do you think I can make it better for him?
THERAPIST: Well, do you think you could tell him about what we talked about today—explain to him that this is how you manage your feelings during separations?

PATIENT: Yeah, because it's not like I don't care.
THERAPIST: No, I don't think so—just the opposite if anything.

PATIENT: That I care too much?
THERAPIST: I think that the intensity of how much you care about people, how you attach to people, drove you to develop this technique. [The therapist had made several attempts to approach the portion of Sylvia's message about mean and hurtful from the standpoint of her being coldhearted. The disruptions that followed may have indicated Sylvia's response to have been more one of feeling accused than of being invited to explore. The therapist now shifts his approach to *his* reading of the message as indicating the intensity of her *positive caring* as the source of her putting people in the "funny place" in "her brain."]

PATIENT: I think you're right. [Pause] It does help to talk about it. It's bothered me for a long time.
THERAPIST: Well, I think the way you have been thinking about it reinforced this idea of you being a coldhearted bitch.

PATIENT: Well, I know I'm not, but people think I am.
THERAPIST: Which really upsets you.

PATIENT: Yeah, but I feel like I don't have any choice to do it before it's done to me.
THERAPIST: How do you mean?

PATIENT: If I do it first, then I don't have it done to me.
THERAPIST: So have other people done this to you?

PATIENT: I don't know because of this mechanism. I think maybe I overuse it—a little bit is OK because it provides me with a little self-protection, but I think I take it too far, and it probably interferes with my relationships with people. [Sylvia is now able to be more reflective, "I think I take it too far," and more open to exploring.]
THERAPIST: So maybe it feels like it keeps you from getting closer to people? [The therapist now moves from the part of the message he has emphasized, Sylvia's coldness, to her emphasis on her loss of connection.]

PATIENT: Sure it does, because to be closer to someone you have to have them in your life, even if they are not there.
THERAPIST: Um-hm.
[Moderately long pause with Sylvia seeming to be comfortably thoughtful]
[During this reflective silence, the analyst recognized that the pattern of a call to connect during a period of absence fit an experience between Sylvia and himself when Sylvia had been away from therapy.]
THERAPIST: Tell me, during our summer break, was this a technique that you used?

PATIENT: Not so much while I was in Europe, but I did use it on the trip to California.
THERAPIST: And how did it go?

PATIENT: You were dead—I mean *gone*. I thought talking in between would help, but it didn't. [Through her metaphor, "dead," Sylvia integrates the two themes of protecting herself against the pain and anguish of missing and the antagonistic coldness, the freezing to death in cold storage of the abandoner.]
THERAPIST: Were you aware of how that contact between trips affected you?

PATIENT: Well, you were gone.
THERAPIST: So talking between trips only upset things?

PATIENT: I guess so. But part of it is right because you were gone—but it only got worse.
THERAPIST: And do you think I went further back into cold storage during the California trip?

PATIENT: Right—but it was OK then because I didn't have to miss you—you were gone. [An additional theme contained in the message about missing was not brought into the foreground. Sylvia could say she felt OK about consciously missing her daughter because she could envision the little girl "happy to be back with her friends." By contrast, Sylvia implies that, unlike her daughter, she does not feel she has been lovingly placed among friends. Moves in her childhood and adult life triggered a belief that she was left unprotected among strangers. She indicates she has felt too upset about abandonment and absorbed in self-protection to open herself to contact and friendship.]

I chose this clinical exchange partially because it is representative of commonplace communications. Nothing dramatic occurs, and nothing dramatic is discussed. Yet when the message containing the message is examined closely, the richness of its complex texture can be recognized. The theme of missing, once identified, helps to give unity to the entire communication. The richness of the message as delivered, however, derives for the many subthemes of past and present experiences that are touched on and from the nature of the interchanges between Sylvia and the therapist. For the most part, they work closely together, but at times he is pushing her to deal with the impact of her withdrawal. The message contained in the message of his linguistic choices, such as "coldhearted bitch," reflects his intensifying the issue he is hoping she will be more willing to explore. Thus, the message contains Sylvia's explicit and implicit communications to him and to herself, his explicit and implicit communications to her and to himself, and the overt and covert pulls and tugs being enacted between them.

REFLECTIONS ON WORDS

The exploratory psychotherapies are about words and relationships. A skeptic might say, "Well, so is life, so what distinguishes therapy?" The communication during exploratory therapy depends on a unique combination of words and relating. The words and the emotions they convey and elicit when exchanged between two people who have no other integral connection with each other makes it possible for a unique relationship to form. The relationship as it forms provides the safety needed for the words of both therapist and patient to convey more directly the thoughts and feelings of each. The relationship as it forms and shifts provides itself a centrally rich source for exploration of what is transpiring between them that requires words to carry out.

Their relationship can bring patient and therapist together with safety, humor, and the sharing of pain and joy. An interpenetration of mind/body states often is achieved through implicit nonverbal communication, but wisdom about one another is enhanced by words. A therapist identifying and designating a feeling or motive a patient is groping to recognize provides the patient with an illuminating focus that the dyad can use to map a whole realm of experience. The theme of "missing" in the session with Sylvia is one example. In another example, I helped a patient to identify that in a series of actions he was taking, the common goal was revenge. Once identified, "revenge" provided a handle to crystallize and organize his thinking. Alternatively, words can form buttresses against organizing thinking if they are used to concretize experience. As an example, a young boy had suffered the painful humiliation of an auditory processing disorder in preschool. Subsequently, he resisted all efforts his parents and teachers made to help him by insisting that he was stupid. This word, having delusionlike intensity and rigidity, offered no opening for consideration. Only his talents for athletics lay outside the wall of impenetrable resistance that consolidated around his universal answer of "No. I'm too stupid!"

What, then, is the distinction between "revenge," which as a designator opened a patient's realm of experience to recognition and discussion and "stupid," which closed down on consideration of past and present experience? First, "revenge" filled the patient's desire to conceptualize his experience and motives with clarity. Second, revenge became useful for therapist and patient to use as a metaphor to link past and present experiences. In contrast, "stupid" had no metaphoric ambiguity for the boy. It was as concrete as if it were a physical weapon used to beat him, and he was using it both to fend off and to wound others. Only through the nonspecific aspects of a therapy relationship and the initially concrete, repetitive use of play could its metaphoric use as a communicative word be restored. A therapist's sensitivity to the nuances of words, and the behavioral communications that accompany them, helps to move understanding from the limitation of concrete usage to the flexibility of metaphor.

In this chapter, I offered the guideline of utilizing as fully as possible the message as delivered. In chapter 5, I will consider further the nature of verbal communication. A patient's narrative account of her experience may be full of those orienting details and specific information that allow for easy comprehension. Unfortunately, a patient's descriptions often are either too terse or too discursive for a therapist's adequate understanding. Filling the narrative envelope is then needed for progress to be made.

CHAPTER 5

FILLING THE NARRATIVE ENVELOPE

DRAWING ON AN ANALOGY TO PLAYS AND NOVELS, to bring a narrative to life requires a context of time, place, and person—the who, what, when, where, and how of an event. Patients tell their story, however in whatever way they will or can and the task falls on therapists to build the narrative to a level of coherence for both. Therapists need to ask who someone is, what was happening in an event that was upsetting, how the patient felt about the choice she made, how old she was at the time, who else was involved, and all of the circumstances leading up to the event.

We all, patient and therapist alike, have a story to tell, but we are not all alike in our ability or willingness to tell it. Sylvia, the patient in chapter 4, was a willing narrator but told her story in brief statements so that she and her analyst developed a pattern of rapid frequent interchanges—a conversational dialogue. As is conventional, Sylvia was principally the teller of the story of sending her daughter to school, taking the steroids, fighting with her husband, and her way to deal with absences. The therapist asked her to tell him what happened, what she felt, what the funny place was like, what was it that she said, did she follow the pattern with her father, was she worried about people seeing her as cold, and did she use the "funny place" technique with the therapist's own absence that summer. All of these questions were to encourage her to fill out the narrative and to orient her to significant issues the therapist believed needed to be expanded. Other interventions had more to do with his attempts to indicate that he heard and understood her, that is, his empathic success in sensing into her message from her point of view. At one point she asks him to be expansive: "Do *you* get it?" In response, they shift roles as teller, and the therapist fills in his narrative of what he has heard and understood. To his question, "Does that seem right," she reassures him that it does, allowing her to resume being the principal narrator.

Sylvia and her therapist evolved a narrative style based largely on Sylvia's proclivity to make brief statements and the value her analyst found in offering her frequent encouraging bridging questions and comments. Each patient–therapist dyad creates a unique dialogue based on the patient's mode of communication when discussing different aspects of her problems and the therapist's personal responsiveness and training. I am advocating an open therapeutic style in sharp contrast to the "silent" analyst of mythic caricature (who unfortunately did exist). It is not for therapists to chat rather than listen, but it is their charge to help their patients in every way they can to reveal the who, what, where, when, and how that is needed for each to enter the scene of the event, memory, dream, or reverie under consideration. This means that therapeutic technique shifts away from peeking between the cracks of free association for a hidden message to elaborate more fully a coherent collaborative depiction of life experiences.

Narrative richness during therapy transcends mere storytelling. To reshape a patient's problem with his identity, therapist and patient must be in touch with the patient's biographic self. The symbolic world that a child forms and lives in is a world of stories. We build stories about going to the zoo, about being at grandmother's apartment, about how father treats mother, about our sister's love and treachery. Our mind is full of stories and, most of all, stories about who we are, who we have been, and who we are going to be. All our stories and scenes, our theater of the mind with our pretends and pretensions, combine to be our autobiography, and our autobiography is coincident with our sense of self. A therapist's attention to a patient's narrative is thus a primary means of gaining entry into the patient's inner sanctum—his private collections of personal experiences, reremembered and coconstructed with the therapist.

Attachment researchers discovered that adults asked to describe their experiences with respect to attachment revealed in the mode of telling the story important clues to the nature of these experiences and to strategies they adopted as children to achieve and preserve the greatest degree of security their attachment experiences allowed. The complex patterns of these behaviors involving approach and avoidance and overt or covert intense emotions often prove analogous to patterns of speech that adults employ when narrating their memories of attachment experiences. This remarkable analogy between a pattern of behavior followed by a preverbal one-year-old infant when seeking the security of attachment and an adult telling about remembered experiences indicates that patterns of narration contain embedded affective memories of presymbolic and symbolic intersubjective experiences. The mode of telling itself contains the story it is telling, at least with respect to attachment experiences and frequently when other motivated experiences are being described. Paradoxically, although the narrative style reveals an essential component of early attachment experiences, the style contributes to serious problems in filling the narrative envelope when the early behavioral strategies produced only an insecure attachment.

Many anxious–resistant infants adopt a strategy with their caregiver of approaching and pushing away. They adopt this ambitendant pattern in response to angry inconsistent parenting. As adults, they present their attitudes with respect to attachment in a form of speech that illustrates their continued preoccupation with the struggles that characterized their childhood attachments. Asked to describe his early experiences with his father a preoccupied speaker might say, "Well he was OK, the old man. He was strict and I was scared of him. My mother said I shouldn't sass him, but I couldn't listen to her because he was always pushing her around. Like when I called home last night and she answered the phone and I thought she had been crying and she told me my sister had called."

The speaker has lost track of the subject with rapid shifts from his answer to the initial question about his father to his mother and from past to present. Because of continued absorption in the troubled relationship he is describing, he sacrifices collaboration to an inner pressure that moves him anxiously away from one troubling topic to another. Narrative clarity requires knowing what was the mother crying about, did it have to do with the father, what role did the sister's call play? To get back to the original subject of the father's strictness and the patient's sassing would require an active effort both to note the moving away and to help the patient to reorient himself.

An example from the analysis of Nancy, recorded in *The Clinical Exchange* (1996, pp. 33–34), demonstrates a similar, less dramatic movement of approach and push away.

"Well, I was pretty mad yesterday. I come back, lie down, and I get mad again. I don't like to be mad. It's so overwhelming. What is going on in here is I take all the responsibility and you get all the fun [chuckling]. Getting so mad about taking all the responsibility destroys the possibility of my living at peace with the world. A fundamental injustice between men and women. I have two choices, deny that it's real, or if it is real, I have to accept it. I don't like the feeling of being manipulated, which is how I feel in here. Not only male–female but the way I see things in general. I feel like I have one foot nailed to the ground while I struggle to do things and the rest of the world moves about freely. [Mildly angry] I had a dreadful thought about you yesterday. My brother would examine things—pull the wings off a fly and watch it squirm, get pleasure—that's what you are doing! You're part of it. You can do nothing about it but make your living off it. I feel like a real misogynist. Before this when I got really angry with you, I could tie myself down [crying] by reminding myself you seem to be a decent man. It doesn't help now. You look benign."

Filling the narrative envelope in an interview requires an interviewer to be aware of what is being omitted and to have the interest and curiosity to request the information. Filling the narrative envelope with a patient immersed in an intensive therapeutic experience requires sensitivity to both the needed information and the affective state of the patient. Especially with a patient who has a preoccupied style of relating her story, the principal theme will be embedded in shifting verbal complexity and more or less obscured as the sense of security in the dyad diminishes or rises. In Nancy's remarks opening the session, differing but interrelated themes abound. She begins and ends with her ambivalent relationship with her therapist. She introduces a central theme of responsibility and couples it with male–female issues (a common coupling for children who have experienced sexual abuse). She refers to her sense of entrapment (being nailed down) and couples it with her brother's sadism. She ends with her puzzlement about the therapist—is he benign and to be trusted or is he deceptive, seductive, and sadistic?

What is the therapist's task with a preoccupied speaker such as Nancy? To make the communication come alive as a dyadic sharing of meaning, the therapist must help Nancy recognize those themes that are salient in the dense, rapidly shifting moving toward and moving away of her narrative. The therapist helps the patient to bring into the foreground for their mutual exploration not omitted details as with a dismissing patient, but emotionally significant stories of self-with-other that are easily lost in the verbal overflow. In selecting themes to take up with patients, I give priority to affective expression, evocative metaphoric imagery, and newly emerging portrayals.

Comparing the response therapists have to preoccupied speech and dismissing speech, we can employ the clichés of "I couldn't get a word in edgewise" or "It's like pulling teeth." More formally we can compare the filling of conversational space by the patient as being too much or too little to be collaborative. Sonya, whose treatment is detailed in *A Spirit of Inquiry*, was on the far end of the spectrum of avoidant patients. Raised in a household comprising a childlike mother who treated every response of Sonya as a repudiation of her own needs, an obsessive, duty-bound father insensitive to feelings, and a disturbed, abusive brother, Sonya entered treatment completely engulfed in depression and pessimism although functioning at a high level professionally. She offered nothing spontaneously, arguing that she had nothing to say and that if she did say something, it would accomplish nothing. Her answers to the therapist's questions were laconic and monosyllabic. Moreover, she averred that any depictions of past experiences were not memories but what she had been told. I believed that she regularly dismissed and disavowed the details and meanings of events in order to function. She sought security by locking herself in her room to keep others out and locking her feelings, thoughts, and memories in her mind, confiding only in a small group of trusted female friends.

For a long time, the sessions followed an unrelenting pattern of long silences, pauses, and extremely sparse speech. Sonya would look at me with an expression of helpless despair and say nothing. I would ask, "How are you feeling?" She would answer "Same" in a flat voice. Remembering that she had described a previous treatment as a dreadful experience in which she had said nothing and the analyst had made no response, I decided to tread a thin line between asking questions to relieve the silence and respecting her aversion to demands to talk revealingly. After her "Same," I allowed a silent interval and observed her with largely a peripheral gaze until I saw an indication of a readiness to be less avoidant. Her head or eyes turning to me, a restless movement of her foot, a change in facial expression would encourage me to ask a further question such as, "How are you sleeping?" "Not well" might be the answer, followed by another silence. After comparable intervals and indications, I might ask about her eating, her work, how she had spent her weekend, and what plans she had for the next weekend. She would respond with pertinent terse answers and would be unresponsive to my "follow-up" questions. I believed, and thought that she believed as well, that the content we exchanged was less important than the effort we were both making to reduce the stress of a tense, empty 45 minutes. My view was that I was tracking her responses as I would a traumatized infant with whom I was attempting to make and preserve a secure contact despite the child's avoidant–dismissive withdrawal.

Gradually Sonya began to add sparse spontaneous comments to her lament about being exhausted and unable to bear it much longer. My relief and joy at her greater involvement was shattered by my recognition that after a more communicative session, she boomeranged into a full-blown avoidant depression. Subsequently she very reluctantly agreed to antidepressant medication and became more able to sustain a narrative exchange. The avoidant–dismissive tendencies now became less global and more embedded in the mode of speech, as in the following session a day after she had taken her professional boards.

Sonya entered and perfunctorily asked how I was, then looked away depressed and exhausted. I noted her tired, sad appearance. She said the boards had been awful, she didn't know how she did, and she didn't care. A dismissive silence followed. I asked, "Going back to work troubling you?"

PATIENT: I'm taking the day off. I couldn't face work.
THERAPIST: I'm glad to see you are looking out for yourself. Last week you took over for others and worked late into the night.

PATIENT: It's not work, it's the boards. My work can give me a feeling of accomplishment; taking the boards gives me none. [This was a mixed message. It included a slightly arrogant negation of my suggestion, a helpful setting us on the right track, an extremely rare admission that her work gave her a feeling of accomplishment, and a bitter complaint about being forced to do something against her will.]
THERAPIST [Seeing an opportunity to fill the narrative envelope]: What was taking the boards like?

PATIENT: Two six-hour days of hell locked up in a room. A lot of questions, many of them stupid. Some were OK. Things I work with all the time. Others were antiquated and I had no idea, so I just put anything down. It was so stupid. It was as if you had to learn the names of all the state capitals in alphabetical order to pass medical boards. [This was a rare acknowledgment of my existence.]
THERAPIST: Oh.

PATIENT: It was stupid!
THERAPIST: A frustrating unnecessary exercise.

PATIENT: I called several friends and they were sympathetic, but it was my own fault—not taking the waiver when I could and

transferring the boards I had taken (previously) and passed. I feel like I was hit by a stick. It's all so stupid. Being asked a lot of stuff you don't need to know. Being kept in a room for two days.
THERAPIST: It sounds like torture.

PATIENT: Um-hmm. [Looking away silently]
[Pause]
THERAPIST: Only you said, "Hit by a stick"—did you mean punished?

PATIENT: [With a burst of anger] What else would it mean?
THERAPIST: It could mean abuse.

PATIENT: Oh. Well, it was both—abuse and punishment—What are you smiling about? [I had smiled involuntarily, and she asked in a way that seemed genuinely curious as well as provocative.]
THERAPIST: I like it when you flare up. You come alive, you become animated, and for a moment you are out of your despair.

PATIENT: Well, maybe I should be a smartass more.
THERAPIST: I know you can be lively with your friends.

PATIENT: I try.
THERAPIST: Do you have to try or sometimes does your liveliness just flow?

PATIENT: Sometimes it flows, but mostly I try. [A silence followed in which I felt that her avoidance had resumed and I would await an initiative from her.]

PATIENT: I had a good experience with my mother. A surprise. She sent me flowers before the boards and called to wish me luck. She never calls me. I have to call her. It was nice of her.
THERAPIST: You were surprised and pleased.

PATIENT: I didn't expect to hear from anyone. Of course, I didn't tell my father.
THERAPIST: What went into your decision not to tell him?

PATIENT: I knew he'd say, "How many times did I tell you to apply for the waiver." I didn't want to hear it.
THERAPIST: You had been hitting yourself with the stick enough —your mother was thinking of your feelings, your father of his advice.

PATIENT: [Defensively] He doesn't know me. I was only a little kid [when her parents were divorced]. He'll ask me about it after a while.

As the session ends, through our exchanges about her mother and father Sonya introduces another theme: the ambivalence I have observed that children of divorced parents often feel. They are flooded with the criticisms that each parent explicitly and implicitly levels against the other. This criticism threatens the child with the loss of an attachment the child may wish to maintain. She can criticize a parent herself as Sonya did her father, but can become protective when someone else (the therapist) echoes the criticism. The ending of this session signaled the existence of another narrative envelope that would need to be opened later.

Mr. N presented another challenge to make communication come alive. He ground through session after session, talking in a tense, forced you-told-me-I-am-to-do-this-so-I'm-doing-it style. Unlike Sonya, who reluctantly provided any detail about her experiences, Mr. N described his life in great detail with the only affect being irritability and sarcasm. At times he would become more tense and constrained, lapsing into prolonged silences. He would hold his chin and have a look of intense, strained concentration—the pose of Rodin's *The Thinker* or of a child straining on the toilet. Efforts to encourage him to describe his feelings at these times failed to help. I became convinced that he lacked sufficient self-awareness of emotion to be more revealing. He experienced my asking him about his feelings as drawing attention to his inadequacy in introspection, rather than being helpful. I resolved to "listen" to the gap in his speech to try to help identify his inner state. After various periods of this "concentration" silence, he began to describe fantasies of blatant aggressive actions, such as being devastatingly sarcastic toward his boss or having people under his power hold a young girl while he sexually assaults and humiliates her. I could successfully take up with him how his rage fantasies arose in response to a specifiable narcissistic slight, but although he could be responsive to the connections I made, he could make no linkages on his own. Specifically, he was unable to process the implications of his fantasies and dreams through the use of analogy and metaphor. I found that when I actively used analogy mixed with a detailed explanation of the links, he readily appreciated and used the information. He began to understand humiliating criticisms, which he had received for years from friends, that he couldn't catch on to a suggestion or to humor based on metaphor.

Another important communicative gap remained. He avoided having and acknowledging a direct feeling or wish toward me as though his very being would be threatened. His conscious fixed placement of me was as a calm, successful man who had it all together and would use his professional skills to help him to get it all together. He was terrified that rage toward me would destroy the equanimity he strove to achieve in the reciprocal envelope of a calm but rigidly formal interaction with me. By focusing on his discontinuities in speech and linking the contents of his fantasies to occurrences between us during the session, I was able to help him appreciate his need to exclude me. A session late in the therapy indicates the progress made in animating this final missing element in Mr. N's ability to communicate his feelings to himself and to the therapist.

Mr. N began by stating with pride that, as a result of the treatment, he resisted a desire to go into a funk at work when he felt resentful. Yet he was disappointed that he still fretted over a minor criticism from his boss. Then, after a typical constrained silence, he reported a fantasy of saying good-bye to a woman colleague whose response was cold and perfunctory. He took a gun and killed her husband. After a further silence, he said he'd like to ignore his fantasy. I noted his wish to treat it as a waste product of his mind to be discarded and ignored as shameful. He agreed and said his action in the fantasy of killing the husband reminded him of his resentment toward his father for not being able to prevent his mother from her cold, cutting ways. I asked him to reflect on his having the fantasy at the particular moment in the session, and he answered that he knew it had a meaning but he couldn't make the connection. I reminded him that, after telling me with pride of what he had accomplished, he had said that he was disappointed at *still* being upset by a small criticism. With feeling, he added, "Oh, I'm angry at you that after all this treatment, I still get upset." He went on to say that when I wasn't responsive to him, like the woman in the fantasy, he gets distant and *irritating*. I said, "irritating." After a brief denial, he acknowledged that he has long known, but felt too much spite to admit, that his silences, his ignoring me, his "self-anesthesia" must be frustrating and irritating to me.

Recapitulating the theme of this chapter, communication comes alive when the narrative envelope is filled with the who, what, where, when, and how of an event. Much more than details are required, however. The vitality of the narrative derives from the expression of emotion, the me-to-you personal involvement of many of the interchanges and the creative use of spontaneity and metaphor. In any session the vitality of the narrative is subject to several factors: the degree of comfort and security patient and therapist feel in dealing with a particular motivation, the status of the comfort and security each feels about their immediate and underlying relationship, and the gains that have been made in the therapy in being open to explore a particular subject.

For example, Professor B had two areas of primary concern: his professional advancement and his troubled marriage. When discussing his problems in his profession, he was articulate, furnished considerable detail, and responded to my requests for additional information. He was relatively open to explore his emotions, although for him this was new territory. In contrast, any mention of his wife was terse and constricted. We had little opportunity to build a narrative beyond knowing of his strong disappointment, his reluctance to recognize how he felt, and how threatening the issue was for him. For a long time we made considerable progress in exploring his problems at work, but he had so compartmentalized his experience that the growth in the one area did not extend into the other. Beyond Professor B's aversion to discussing his marriage, a difference in the emotional feel of our working together presented another factor. His approach to our exploring his professional problems was cooperative and collaborative, whereas he responded to efforts I made to enter into a discussion of his marriage with a subtle hostility that I could sense but did not understand.

A crisis in their family forced his attention to focus on disturbances in their communication. I learned that in his wife's presence Professor B was shut down in both speech and affect. She monitored everything he said, and, with a critical glance from her, he became silent, withdrawn, and drowsy. In addition, for years she had served as his "psychological" advisor. This led to two influences on his narrative flow with me. First, the fear of loss of this dependence inhibited his willingness to open himself to the full extent of his dissatisfaction. Second, largely out of his awareness, he had set up a competition between his wife and me. This "enactment" (see chapter 7) of being played off against his wife as "counselor" was the source of the tension I felt but didn't understand. Now in the sessions, he expanded the narrative about their relationship and became as responsive to my efforts to fill the narrative envelope as he was and had been about his work. He began to apply the sensitivity, insight, and intuition that he had freed up in his relationships at work to his interactions with wife and their family crisis. Having entered couples therapy, he and his wife were helped to further repair their disturbed communication as he emerged from an emotionally costly, submissive dependence.

A further example illustrates changes in narrative flow occurring in a single session. I use excerpts from a session of the treatment of P reported extensively by James Fosshage (1990). P's childhood had been traumatic with a fragile, explosively tyrannical father and a mother who couldn't cope with P's ordinary needs and who developed a severe paranoid disturbance. In the preceding sessions, P had become very upset by an inadvertent discovery that she interpreted as evidence that her analyst was not the strong, confident person she had believed him to be. P begins the session describing her helpless feeling about being in a relationship "because I feel so threatened by anybody's needs. And lots of human beings are around me—my son, my friends, my family . . ."

ANALYST: Your analyst.
P: My analyst . . .

ANALYST: And your reaction when we feel needy?
[The analyst fills the narrative envelope by including himself. This reference to himself might be a diversion were it not that his presumed neediness was directly under consideration as the source of P's distress in the previous hour. At a prior time, the view of him as needy would not have fit at all. Now her omission of him in the list of needy people is an example of a momentary dismissive narrative.]
P: remains dismissive, stating (with a tone of disparagement), "It's so extreme." [Note the impersonal pronoun "it."]

The analyst continues to try to help P with her depressive state and her constrictive narrative. He reminds her of the neediness and suffering around her during her growing up "and understandably you became fearful and intensely reactive when you sense neediness in others today." P responds that she knows that, implying the analyst's reminders about her past as a generalized communication can be experienced as more condemning than helpful. With a more open appeal, however, she asks, "but how am I going to change?" The analyst alters his narrative to become more specific. He suggests that as she reviews her experiences with him, she "will be able gradually to experience other's neediness and pain as not *so* frightening and unmanageable." He reminds her of her success in a dream of taking care of herself "by actively choosing not to take care of the other." Encouraged, she asks, "You really think so?" and he answers, "Yes, I really do."

P: pauses and then says, "It was very helpful for me [with a more energetic tone] to be able to tell you, to feel that I could tell you the things I despise about you. That I felt you weren't strong enough. You see [emphatically] I don't tell B [her husband]. I don't tell my father. I don't tell people. . . . I think it is very helpful to tell you that and know you won't fall apart. I was afraid I hurt you, but . . . that was a new thing for me actually to be able to tell you. And you're still here and [with laughter] not dead."

With only several uh-huhs and a few words of encouragement from the analyst, P carries the narrative forward throughout the remainder of the session. She takes up an exploration of her present attitude, a traumatic experience at age three with her mother and her loss of the idealized view of the analyst. At times, the narrative flow threatens to falter as P momentarily becomes preoccupied with shifts in setting, time, and person. Through shared humor playfulness, however, and the analyst's simple interventions, P maintains an openness to explore. After a reflective pause, she states, "I'm feeling I don't know where things are going from here. I came in feeling they were not to go anywhere. Now, I'm just feeling that I don't know and that's sort of all right. I'm calm about that. . . ."

Once reflection enters a patient's (or a therapist's) narrative flow, the message is bidirectional: to the other and from and to the self. A narrative envelope that contains all the elements needed for both telling and reflection offers a richer, more vital quality to a story-being-told.

To state the obvious, all elements of a story-being-told are not of equal significance to therapists engaged in exploring meanings and motivation. In this chapter, I have taken up aspects of a narrative needed for a listener to enter into the mind state of a speaker. In the next chapter I will describe the importance of attributions patients make about their therapists.

CHAPTER 6

"THE WEARING OF ATTRIBUTIONS"

A GUIDELINE FOR THERAPISTS TO DISCOVER WHO THEY HAVE COME TO BE FOR THEIR PATIENTS

THIS PRINCIPLE OF TECHNIQUE CRYSTALLIZED for me when I found myself repeatedly telling therapists whom I supervised, "You are searching for the patient's latent message to discover the transference, the who that the patient unconsciously and consciously regards you to be. All the while you ignore or fail to utilize the opportunity available to you through the patient's overt or implied attributions about you. You should 'wear these attributions.'" From infancy on, humans follow a particular pattern in giving meaning to relationships. Infants detect salient features of emotion stirring interactional sequences and develop categories for similar repeated events such as feedings or "conversational" playing. As attachment research attests, by one year of age infants distinguish between a familiar caregiver and a stranger and have a clear category of expectations of how their caregiver is likely to respond to their entreaties and distress. Once they enter the realm of symbolic processing, toddlers draw inferences from their intersubjective experiences. Parents have long held a view of who their baby is to them: a very special little girl just like her mother, or a burdensome, demanding whiner. Now child and parents use their experiences with one another to create identities that typify their lives together. Each person uses the mirroring they receive from the other to stabilize their identity and to regulate their interactions. This process of finding oneself in the mind of the other becomes a central feature of exploratory therapies. I have called the guideline that facilitates therapists locating and accepting who they have come to be in the minds of their patients the "wearing of attributions."

The wearing of attributions, as I illustrate, involves therapists' recognizing an attribution made about them and then attempting to regard their selves as portrayed in the attribution. Once therapists listen to their patients and themselves from the perspective of the attribution, a unique, highly revealing dialogue often ensues.

The example of Nancy's preoccupied speech in chapter 5 included a number of attributions about me that proved central to the issues we were exploring. "I take all the responsibility and you get all the fun." "I don't like the feeling of being manipulated, which is how I feel in here." "My brother would examine things—pull the wings off a fly and watch it squirm and get pleasure. That's what you are doing! You're part of it. You can do nothing about it but make your living off it." "Before this when I got really angry with you I could tie myself down [crying] by reminding myself you seem to be a decent man. It doesn't help now. You look benign."

My first task in wearing these attributions was to wonder how my presumed sadistic malevolence could be combined with a deceptive (seem to be) appearance of benignity. What picture of myself was being held up to me that would fit a benign appearance with a malevolent intent? I suggested, "If my very presence and my benign appearance invite your interest and curiosity, does that become a part of the problem?"

Nancy and I then focused on her sense of the unfairness of having all responsibility placed on her and women for men's actions. Nancy then added a further attribution: "Another strange thing in this is all related to your going away. For the last 24 hours, I've been aware I won't see you for two weeks. I had real ambivalent—not ambivalent; I want you to go! Not to have to come here and talk. Out of sight, out of mind. As long as you're here, I have to deal with whatever my unsuccessfully repressed fantasies are." Returning to the opening attribution, I said, "Absent I'm not an invitation for your fantasies and feelings."

PATIENT: Right [pause]. I'm not at all certain you're not just an awful human being. Who are you? Am I doing the right thing by coming? Can I trust you? Yet I find myself not wanting to be separated from you. Whatever you are, it's better than being alone. I hate myself for that. I hate you for not being one or the other—good or bad. I seem not to be able to deal with the notion that you are human, not perfect.
THERAPIST: In the imperfections you experience me as having, is the one about my going away the most problematic at this time?

PATIENT: I don't know. I wouldn't have said that was necessarily an imperfection—I don't want to admit that's it. I did think of it, that's true, but I don't want to admit that separations are as distressing as they are. I get so angry at you and at me. What is wrong is I feel so dependent. Yet I'm frightened when you go away, I want to hang on so tight. I want to say you aren't worth the allegiance. I'm so mad. It catches you up again and again. I'm no better off. You let me be—or don't stop me from being dependent. I think with a sick feeling in my stomach of what happened in January or February when you were gone. [Nancy had gotten into serious trouble by gossiping about a student she knew had cheated on a test.] I pointed out the girl to my friend, told her she's the girl who cheated.
THERAPIST: You're feeling I'm responsible for letting you down.

PATIENT: I'm going to say my problem with your being benign is I try to trust you—things will be okay—and they aren't, and then it's my problem.
THERAPIST: We also looked at your feeling that I cheated. I tempt you to trust me and then I go away.

PATIENT: [Crying] I'm the one who has to stay and take care of things while you're gone. Make mistakes. I hate you for going

> away and doing that. The same way I hated my mother. I have a vision of getting up and throwing everything in this room at you. A barrage of stuff. That's what I'm doing right now.

Throughout this session, I tried to envision myself as Nancy portrayed me through her attributions. In general, Nancy made it easy for me because of the clarity of her attributions. And much of Nancy's view of me did not seem foreign: I did invite her trust, and I did leave her in states of distress when I went away. I did not see myself as a sadistic puller-off of wings, although I could recognize myself as someone who might at times insist on "exploring" even if it contributed to the patient's momentarily feeling she was being treated like an "object." Often I or any therapist opening himself to how he is conceived of in the patient's mind will learn about aspects of himself he either hadn't recognized or, if he did, didn't believe he was revealing.

Who, then, is the therapist? Nancy sees similarities to her brother and father, who invited and then betrayed her interest and trust and then blamed her for it. She also sees me as similar to her mother, who invited and then betrayed her trust and dependence by going away on visits to her family, leaving Nancy unprotected "to take care of things" (keep house) for the men and "make mistakes," that is, get into sexual activities with her brother. The attributions are about who I am to Nancy in the present. Her view of me in the here and now is, however, entwined with significant figures in her past. This brings us to a discussion of transference.

TRANSFERENCE

Psychoanalysis received one of its greatest revelations when Freud discovered that his patients were reacting to him in a manner disparate to his actual identity and then found that they were projecting onto him unconscious repressed aspects or attributes of their important childhood figures. Freud believed the energy that characterized the early relationship was transferred to the analytic relationship with him. This discovery of transference, an influence arising from the past affecting a present relationship, was momentous for psychoanalysis. Freud's further conception was that the attributes of the parents projected onto an analyst were based not on the actual parents or events but on distortions created by the primitiveness of sexual and aggressive drives. The explanatory value of drive distortion has proven less convincing and is, I believe, supplanted by our current account of development. In a current account, lived experience arises out of multidimensional systems of motivation organized by mutual and self-regulation, is propelled by positive and negative affective expression of self with others, and is constrained by limitations in cognitive capacities in the presymbolic and early symbolic periods.

From the earliest moments, infants organize, categorize, and generalize their lived experience. The patterns of self with other that characterize these lived experiences lead the child to form expectations. Good experiences of self with other lead a child to expect that she will have other similar good experiences. Children invariably have enough disappointments, however, to know that bad experiences can be expected, too. Children who have had significantly bad experiences of self with other develop a dread, an often fatalistic and pessimistic expectation, that comparable bad experiences will befall them. Alternatively, most children, no matter how abused or neglected, have enough good experiences or fantasies of them to have an overt or latent expectation that this time it will be different. Without some hope that life can be better, treatment cannot be successful. These two-sided expectations that take the form, respectively, of good again but sometimes bad, or bad as usual but this time maybe different, tilt the perspective of everyone (patient and therapist).

This view of biphasic expectations directly contradicts the positivist objectivist conception that dominated thinking at the time Freud discovered transference. Freud reasoned that an analyst's neutrality and abstinence would allow him to present himself as a blank screen to his patient. The patient would then have imprinted on the screen the identity, behaviors, and attitudes of a past significant figure as veridical as a photographic image. I believe no exploratory therapist could or should want to be a blank screen, certainly Freud never was. Rather, a therapist is and must be an active, affectively present individual. Therapists are continuously communicating aspects of themselves through their speech, silence, accent, posture, chair squeaks, clothing, breathing, remembering, forgetting, reliability, absences, illnesses, office décor, jewelry, "ums," grunts, stomach noises, walking pace, and, most important, the ups and downs of their affective expression. In fact, rather than a blank screen, hundreds of cues emanate from therapists all the time, explicit and implicit, known to them or unknown, and constantly changing in response to altered contexts presented by the patient and by the exigencies of their own lives. A patient is consciously or unconsciously searching for and registering cues that confirm or contradict a positive or negative expectation. For Nancy, the slightest nuance of condescension in my voice, a tone unrecognized by me until I "wore" the attribution, could send her into a frenzy of righteous indignation. In a further erosion of an illusion of objectivity, we find that quite minor cues patients identify can lead to greater-than-anticipated reactions, whereas larger occurrences on either side, such as an act of kindness or an analyst's mixing up an appointment time, may have little effect.

From some perspective of the patient, the therapist's presence and influence is omnipresent. At all times, the therapist-in-the-patient's-mind is categorized on a spectrum of a secure to insecure base. This placement on the spectrum exerts a background influence regulating the cues sought in the foreground. In addition, a patient's current life experiences and the therapist's overt and covert communications tilt the patient's focus toward or away from the therapist and specific attributions about him.

CLINICAL EXAMPLES

Jacqueline was in an ending phase of a successful exploratory treatment. She and her husband were in a period of considerable stress—she with sick children, and he with his career. They generally got along very well, an outcome she attributed to her treatment, which had enabled her no longer automatically to anticipate insensitivity, abandonment, and denial from others. Our relationship was also generally friendly and collaborative. From the beginning of the therapy, I had consistently taken up any disruptions and breach between us and tried to engage her in describing and acknowledging the sources for her that arose in the treatment. The session I present to illustrate my "wearing" of an emerging transference attribution followed a weekend in which she and her husband had been unusually testy with each other.

> PATIENT: Boy, I need to come today. Ben (her husband) and I are at a low ebb—maybe the lowest. He is coming home late and keeps getting work calls when I need him to help me with the children. Then he says I should manage better and I was unfair to want him to give up his Sunday tennis. I say he should work less. He says we need the money and started asking me about my personal credit card. We kind of made up and were lying in bed when he said maybe you ought to get your sister to come and help you, and I can go away for a short trip. I thought, where is that coming from? No! He wants to leave me. Not *we* go away, but him. He's never said that before. I was shocked. I started to think—he wants to get away from me. I've done something wrong, and he's punishing me. That's my mother, that's not Ben. So I tried to control myself and I really do believe it's OK for him to go away himself with his friends. I'm glad he has friends. But I couldn't contain it. I felt so hurt. [An unusually long pause followed.] Where are you? You usually have something to say, to help me.
>
> I was startled by the attribution—where are you? Have you left me too? Something is happening that is unusual. I have come to expect you to take up problems, to help me see aspects of myself I'm not seeing. For me her attribution was accurate in one respect: I had left her in that I was not seeing the experience as presenting the threat she viewed it to be.
>
> THERAPIST: You're right. I have not been with you in the way I usually am. My view has been too different.
>
> PATIENT: Well tell me. I need to hear it whether I'm going to like it or not.
>
> THERAPIST: OK. As you described what Ben said, I heard a hus-

band who felt overworked and troubled spinning out a daydream of escape.

PATIENT: Oh, you didn't hear him just wanting to get away from me. I felt that so strongly even though I told myself that's not Ben. But we had such an awful weekend of not getting along. [Pause] What were you hearing? A day dream? Just to have a time out? [Both curious and skeptical]
THERAPIST: You might be skeptical about me. I did abandon you in a sense—or abandon sharing your view and concern.

PATIENT: OK. Help me see what's happening. I'm having trouble.
THERAPIST: I think the difficulty you are describing arises out of the feeling of stress you and Ben are both feeling so that rather than one helping the other as you have come to expect, you are each trying to protect the areas of sanctuary and autonomy you have left. So over the weekend you started to attack his doing his athletics, and he was getting on you about spending. After these territory battles started, you couldn't hear Ben having an escape fantasy but only the relentless battling with your mother that had been so personalized and wounding.

The remainder of the session was devoted to exploring the way Jackie had dichotomized disagreements into turf wars with no empathy for the position of either by the other but rapid entry into paranoidlike thinking. She reported the next session how she had used humor and understanding to help Ben out of his irritable state as they playfully talked about when each might go for an escape adventure. She dreamt about being in a wonderful store with an older couple who, although her parent's age, were jolly and easy to talk to and who sold her wonderful things and even gave her an unexpected gift. She easily recognized and acknowledged that the attribution presented through the dream imagery referred to the prior session.

In the vignette from Jackie's therapy, the therapist wore the attribution in the form of recognizing and acknowledging that he had "left her" actually and metaphorically. The example of Nick, treated by Frank Lachmann and reported in *The Spirit of Inquiry*, describes an analyst wearing an attribution through an imagined confirmation expressed in humor. Nick was a dependent, isolated gay man who was easily wounded, prone to shame and humiliation, and subject to severe outbursts of self-defeating rage. The analyst was extremely sensitive to Nick's frequent failures in affect regulation and his difficulty with bodily and sexual tensions. "He had a raucous sense of humor, which occasionally broke through his clouds of despair. At those times I would respond in kind, and, for a while, we were able to sustain a playful tone" (2002, p. 61). In one session, Nick was struggling with his shame about his sexuality. "He wondered what I do in my office when I'm alone. He spoke of his 'jerking off' and imagined me in my bathroom 'jerking off with *The Psychoanalytic Quarterly*.' I said, 'Oh, you mean because it has all those pictures?'" (p. 66).

A complex communication was condensed in the analyst's humorous wearing of the attribution. The analyst's empathic understanding was that Nick was trying to construct a sense of commonality with his revered analyst. If they were both masturbaters, Nick would not have to feel such terrible shame. Seen in this light, the analyst wore the attribution by offering an imagined self "jerking off" in response to the stimulation of erotic pictures. Further, they had cocreated a twinship of ironic comedy based on the absurdity of the dry, intellectual abstraction of a technical journal as the equivalent of pornographic literature—the popular caricature of psychoanalysts and their journals as preoccupied with sex.

As with any other response to a patient, a therapist wearing an attribution has many possible ways to communicate. He might have interpreted his explicit understanding of Nick's meaning. Lachmann states, "Interpreting 'you want to make me similar to you' might have been a betrayal of the spirit of our ongoing communication. I would have suddenly left my somewhat ambiguous position in a 'play space' with Nick and differentiated and distinguished myself as the *analyst*" (p. 66).

Mary Jane (referred to in chapter 3) regularly voiced her attributions. In fact, her reference to problems and doubts emanating from me were so frequent they often furnished the most dynamic moments in the session. Not unexpected from her childhood emotional and sexual abuse, she was inordinately sensitive to negative cues. To help her recognize her selective filter, I offered her the analogy of a person driving across the city. The person gets to a red light and fumes, "Damn it, why do I have a red light? Why do I have to stop? I'm in a hurry." The light changes. She drives through three green lights still fuming until she comes to another red light. This triggers another rant. "Why do I get nothing but red lights? How can I get anywhere when I have to put up with this unfairness?"

After a brief pause, she said, "That's not an analogy! That's exactly how it is when I drive." With this sensitivity to negative cues, Mary Jane picked up any sign of my wavering interest, or annoyance, or skepticism. For example, she might tell a story about an event with so great an overload of detail that my attention would flag. "You're bored with me" would follow. I would answer that my attention had been high when she started telling me about what her friend had said when he picked her up. My attention was sustained through some of the detail about their argument about which movie to go to. But then the details about the relative distance to the two theaters left me dropping out.

At times she would get carried away by her anger and make accusations about coworkers sabotaging her. She would recall that she had been told by a previous therapist whom she had trusted that her raging got under people's skin. Nonetheless she would expostulate about what this and that coworker had done. I noted she had remembered her therapist's reference to her raging before she told me about the coworkers' maliciousness.

She talked on about the coworker and then abruptly said, "You're angry with me!"

I acknowledged that when she offers a potentially useful association and drops it even after I remind her, I do feel disappointed and sometimes annoyed, but what did she pick up about me?

PATIENT: It's not what you said. I expected that. It was your tone.
THERAPIST: My tone? [Trying to hear my voice]

PATIENT: Yes, not your usual soft tone but hard, cold, matter-of-fact, no sympathy.

THERAPIST: [Hearing that in my voice as I replay my comment to myself] OK, I can hear that.

PATIENT: You wouldn't use that tone if you weren't really angry.
THERAPIST: I don't know. I wouldn't go that far. I draw a distinction between when I'm annoyed and *really* angry.

PATIENT: I guess you can. I can't, and I wish I could.

ACCEPTANCE, TRANSPARENCY, AND ACCEPTABILITY

To disclose or not to disclose? Answers analysts have given to this question have varied greatly over time. No disclosure was recommended when anonymity was regarded as a necessary safeguard so that transference attributions would arise solely from the patient's experience uncontaminated by knowledge of the analyst. Some disclosure was recommended when analysts were encouraged to demonstrate a "physicianly attitude" (Stone, 1961). For Stone it seemed natural for analysts to answer impersonal questions such as where they were going on vacation. Much more open disclosure is recommended now when the therapists' authenticity, or being "real," is regarded as a necessary ingredient of the type of relationship that is a foundation for exploration. But now the question shifts to what to disclose? My answer is whatever helps to elucidate what is being experienced in the dyadic relationship. A therapist is both an active participant in an intersubjective exploration and an observer and interpreter of the process. A developmental perspective helps to explain my answer.

The security of all relationships is based first on acceptance of the other. Parents prepare to accept their baby long before birth. Mothers gain a sense of their baby's acceptance of them as the baby accepts their mother's feeding and other ministrations. Then with the delight of a glow each parent reads acceptance in the baby's smile. This process of experiencing acceptance or, unfortunately, lack of acceptance continues throughout life and lays the foundation for expectations that play out in therapy.

How do babies or mothers, patients or therapists, know they are really being accepted? Each member of the dyad must be sufficiently transparent to the other. Caregivers start this process by making themselves far more transparent to babies than they are aware. They tell their baby, "I know and accept you when you want to play or be left alone, need to suck or sleep, hate to be diapered, or like teddy as your favorite toy." They tell in actions, but also they tell in words, the importance of which we have only come to realize. They chatter, they label, they praise, they criticize. "Oh you don't want any more." " That's a lovely smile." "Don't pull Mommy's glasses off again." They reveal what's on their mind and what they believe is on their baby's mind. So babies enter the world of their own verbal usage having all kinds of information in deeds and words about themselves and their caregivers. Strong research evidence supports the view that when mothers recognize accurately their infant's mental life and comment on it using mental state language, their children will perform well at age four on tasks that identify the mental states of others. Alternatively, mothers who comment inappropriately on their child's affective mental life and who inaccurately treat a baby's emotion as referencing them have children who rate low on recognition of the mind states of others and also have a high incidence of adolescent dissociative symptoms. Stated simply, mothers who make themselves known to their infants as able to enter the affective mental state of their babies have children who can enter the mind-states of others and themselves. They provide a transparency, an open book of their own and their baby's emotional life together; they enable their children to open the book on themselves and others.

These studies on the significance of maternal revelation about mental states provide the basis for therapeutic transparency. Just as parents can promote their children's capacity for accurate sensing into the mental state of others and themselves, therapists, through their disclosure of what they are recognizing, feeling, and thinking, encourage patients to be more effectively reflective. Therapists accomplish this first through their willingness to reveal what they learn from their empathic entry into their patient's affective mental state; second, through their openness to reveal their own mental state as demonstrated by wearing attributions; and third, through their openness to recognize and identify the affective state of the ambiance they and their patient together have cocreated.

Transparency, revelation, and disclosure by patient or therapist are not without risk. Each may find what he or she has learned about the other to be unacceptable. Early in my training, in accordance with my supervisor's instruction, I refused to accept a small gift from a patient at Christmas, revealing to her and to me a rigid authoritarian potential in me. The patient reacted with pain and rage, and for a very long time all positive feeling was lost. Although we were able to connect the injury to her mother's repeated rejections of the patient's efforts to please her, her sense of being injured by me lingered. Happily the therapy ended well, but years later, at a chance meeting, the patient thanked me for the help but reminded me of my "unforgivable" error. Sometimes the unacceptable discovery can be resolved by a broadening of perspective. Sometimes an impasse or stalemate occurs, or worse, a disruption of the treatment. If the continuity can be retained, revelations by one or both can lead to changes that significantly move the therapy forward and add to the mature self-knowledge of both participants. My experience is that when a therapeutic relationship has developed a background of safety, the uproar from an "unacceptable" disclosure in the foreground can be contained and resolved with more generosity and tolerance from either partner than might have been expected. Early in her therapy, Mary Jane responded with wounded outrage to any small or large failure on my part to be fully responsive to her, such as being a minute late by her clock. As she gradually, over a long time, built up a background feeling of my reliability and empathic understanding of her struggles, she could bring into our exchanges a mutual consideration of her experience of errors on my part, such as a confusion in scheduling or a lapse in my attentiveness.

In chapter 1, I suggested guidelines for making arrangements to begin an exploratory therapy. The next chapters are devoted to guidelines about how therapists listen. Chapter 2 describes the overarching principle of empathic listening, that is, therapists deriving from patients' communications information about patterns of experience, intentions, and meanings as seen largely from the patients' own perspective. Chapters 3, 4, and 5 provide more focused guidance to therapists' listening, indicating priorities for attending and understanding the message. In chapter 3, I emphasize the importance of discerning the emotional component of communications to perceive the nature of a patient's experiences and intentions. In chapter 4, I present the guideline that the message as delivered by the patient verbally and nonverbally is the primary focus of empathic perception. "The message contains the message" guides therapists toward the fullest possible extraction of meaning from a patient's overt explicit communication with all its implicit complexity, rather than regarding the message as a screen obscuring a hidden secret. Chapter 5 guides therapists toward obtaining all the information needed for patients' narratives to come alive as a revealing rendering of their experiences, especially those experiences that have been and are deeply touching to them.

In the remaining five chapters, I shift from guidelines for therapists to listen actively to guides for therapists' active participation, their stepping out onto the "stage" of the "theater of the mind." Chapter 6 presents guidelines for therapists to respond to overt and covert attributions that patients make about them. As therapy moves forward, subtle changes occur in the nature of self with other (patient with therapist, therapist with patient). For exploratory therapies to proceed, therapists need to discover who they have become for their patients, and "wearing the patient's attribution" is critical to their aspect of the inquiry.

The guidelines in this chapter have focused on the identity of therapists as viewed by their patients and as potentially enlarging therapists' view of themselves. In chapter 7, I shift the focus from patients or therapists to experiences they have created between them. An analogy can be drawn between these experiences and dramas or enactments that are sometimes easily recognized, but more often are puzzling. A guideline to their understanding and exploration is the joint creation of "model scenes."

CHAPTER 7

MODEL SCENES: A GUIDE TO BRINGING THE THEATER OF THE MIND ONTO THE PATIENT–THERAPIST STAGE

AN ANALOGY HAS OFTEN BEEN DRAWN BETWEEN the psyche and theater or stage. Terms such as "schema," "map," "scene," "story," "script," and "relational interactive pattern" have been used to depict the dynamic workings of the brain and a conscious and unconscious experiential mind. "The complex picture of a brain creating an ever-changing individualistic picture of a world full of personal meaning coincides with our sense of a self experiencing an integrated and orchestrated stream of consciousness" (Lichtenberg, Lachmann, and Fosshage, 2002, p. 15). Developmentalists suggest that the individualistic picture of a world of personal meaning forms as memories of events of affective significance to an infant and toddler. "Mommy baked cookies. I eated." Many times a patient's narrative holds closely to the event as remembered with the individuals involved, its sights, sounds, and smells, and the emotions evoked. Other times what is communicated is less an event narrative and more a generalized outlook or feeling state, an accumulated good-naturedness or irritability, optimism or pessimism, courage or apprehension, pride or shame. The mode of communication may be telling in explicit words or enacting through procedural memory.

When listening and reacting to an explicit narrative therapists often have little difficulty orienting themselves to the message being conveyed and to the patient's point of view as he conveys it. Frequently, however, messages are implicit rather than explicit, procedural actions rather than verbal, and nonlinear rather than linear. Consequently, therapists are momentarily or more persistently puzzled and uncertain about the meaning of a communication such as an unexpected involvement in which they find themselves during the ongoing verbal interchanges. Listening may further clarify momentary puzzlement. A dream or association may provide a metaphor that links an action to a patient's symptom or attitude or to unexpected feelings and behavioral responses building up in the therapist.

For extended periods of time, I have found myself perplexed about particular experiences and interchanges I was having with a patient. A notion of these experiences, sometimes unformulated, would "sit" in my mind waiting and loosely searching for an explanation. I found that in time my undirected listening for a key to open the door to the puzzle of what was transpiring between the patient and me was rewarded by the revelation of a scene. The scene might be in the form of a memory; a dream; a description of a movie, play, or book; or a rendering of an event from a prior session. Generally the revelation came from the patient with my recognizing its significance. On rare occasions, the revelation originated from my self-analysis. Whatever its source, I treated my "aha" experience with the skepticism I had been trained to value. I then offered the patient a suggestion in as open a manner as my enthusiasm allowed. I then listened to the patient's response. Was the image or picture I had in my mind from the scene in the memory, dream, movie, or prior session a model that linked organically to something puzzling between us? Happily, my conjecture often has been confirmed by the type of yes and no I value: yes that makes general sense, but no it's not exactly how I see it. We then play puzzle solvers, modifying, adding, and discarding. I refer to coconstructing and cocreating a puzzle-solving depiction that helps to discover the meaning of a significant event or enactment a "model scene."

"Model" addresses the manner in which the scene stands for or exemplifies a metaphoric linkage to, or basis for, an experience that is playing out in the present. "Scene" addresses the manner in which the descriptors can be visualized by therapist and patient and observed from a number of changing viewpoints. Therapist and patient become codirectors staging and restaging the scene as its potential range of explanatory power increases. A dyadic significance beyond explanation accrues to many model scenes. Patient and therapist experience these model scenes as prized joint property, something they have achieved together and can share whenever either feels it is useful. In this way, these particular model scenes become similar to family stories that take on a mythic quality: the time when we all sat together in the hospital not knowing whether father would recover; or the time when the skipper of the boat we charted surprised us with a Passover meal. Family myths, like cultural myths, are told and retold. Their significance lies not primarily in their historical accuracy but in their communal meaning at the time of their retelling. In therapy, constructing model scenes brings events from the theater of the patient's mind into the dyadic experience of events patient and therapist have puzzled over and shared.

CASE EXAMPLE

In chapter 5, I described the difficulty of bringing Mr. N's narrative to life. His I'm-doing-my-duty recitation, his general absence of any spontaneously felt emotion, his irritability and sarcasm in response to any question, his resistance to change, his long silences replete with fantasies of vengeful actions, and his posture of chin-on-hand, intense, strained concentration presented a challenge to understand. I could easily make several preliminary inferences. Mr. N's constricted, strained concentration appeared more likely to be related to specific problems of bowel training than simply a consequence of an anxious–resistant early attachment strategy. Further, I inferred that he had sustained a traumatic disturbance, probably implicating his mother. Serious problems with his mother were suggested by the referring physician, a friend of his family. He strongly urged Mr. N to undergo analysis because of the physician's fear that Mr. N was in danger of a serious entanglement with a woman who was "as paranoid as his mother."

Three model scenes helped to unravel puzzling features of Mr. N's peculiar restrictive communication. The first was cocreated around a "confession" that Mr. N announced blandly in the beginning of his treatment. He had climbed under the piano to defecate until age six or seven. This was stated along with other transgressive acts of stealing and cheating. Together the transgressive actions pointed to a source of rebellious obstinacy and an intense need to suppress overt oppositional stances that might have developed during the bowel training period with a mother characterized as "paranoid."

The second model scene was triggered by a series of recurrent dreams in which Mr. N walked in water where there were snakes and other frightening creatures. These dreams promised help in understanding the fear that froze Mr. N into rigidity.

The third model scene pointed in a different and more positive direction. It was suggested by Mr. N's memories of Freddy, his much-loved, lively dog. These rarely mentioned memories helped to unlock an alternative to the shut-down, frightened Mr. N of the other two model scenes, a Mr. N capable of fondness and animation.

The possibility or more, as I believed, probability of disturbed bowel elimination regulation in toilet training having become emblematic of more general domination–submission proclivities provided a theme that I followed in organizing my understanding of several manifestations. One was his frequent struggles with his mother. He would approach her with his worries, and she would get increasingly nervous and despairing, finally offering him Valium. Any disagreement with her led to a bossy, controlling rejection, and persistence could lead to a hysterical episode with persecutory fears. The push–pull of an anxious–resisting interplay was a regular feature of our interchanges when he would dump out confessions and complaints and reject as wrong, unhelpful, or injurious comments I made in response. A helpful comment might be acknowledged but rapidly led to a complaint about its insufficiency. This paralleled his mother having helped him when he was foundering in school; with her help he made good grades. Then she stopped, and, left on his own, he collapsed in a funk. All of this pointed to a major disturbance in attachment with resulting characterological aversiveness and periods of devitalization, but it did not suggest anything specific about the regulation of elimination that would help explain the symptom of defecating under the piano.

The fearful dreams of walking in water containing snakes and other frightening creatures suggested toilets, but the associations first went in another direction. Mr. N's brother Jay, three years older, became seriously ill with nephritis when Mr. N was three, and his mother had a series of deaths in her family. The level of anxiety was further heightened in the family by Mr. N's father's business failures and litigiousness. Over the course of time, the picture of rigid, fear-driven avoidance filled out. In junior high school, he was terrified to take showers. Everyone assumed it was embarrassment about nudity, but it was the water. He would try not to get wet. He was frightened of swimming but more frightened of the humiliation his brother endured in high school for not being able to get in the pool. He pictured me as highly critical of him for not immersing himself in analysis. I suggested that we understood his reluctance to mean that if he immersed himself fully, he feared he would be hooked to me as he had been to his mother. But what about shower and water? He said he could only think of disease, of his mother's warning against drinking from fountains. He would never touch a fountain.

The next hour, he mused about when he started being afraid of fountains. Was it when he was 10 or 11 or earlier? At three or four, he only knew his brother had nephritis, a kidney disease. That's all. Well, he added, he remembered hearing a story about the doctor who did the wrong thing, and Jay almost died. I suggested that he might have become frightened of whatever in his little-boy mind he may have associated with Jay's illness. He answered, "Nothing I know of" in a tone of openness and appeal. To myself I reflected on the inhibiting effect the experience of ineffectiveness and inadequacy his barriers had so often triggered in me. At this moment, we seemed free of that enactment. I suggested, "Possibly something to do with a doctor who didn't know what he was doing, and things to do with streams and flows and toilets." He said, "I feel it strikes a memory," and after a brief silence he said he remembered his mother complaining that Jay's son wasn't yet toilet trained at two. Her boys, she bragged to him, had been trained long before. He added that it was ironic something that started so well should then prove to be the source of so much trouble.

He then described feeling confused. He wondered if he had gotten all mixed up about disease and toilets and water—perhaps feces, too. I responded that he may have gotten frightened about anything to do with the toilet and tried to avoid it as though it were connected with disease and danger. Excitedly, he replied, "Knowing my mother, she would never have had the patience to explain it." I asked if he pictured her reacting as he had assumed I would—getting agitated and saying you refuse to immerse yourself. "Yes, yes—that I'm stubborn, bad." I added, "Then your concern about disease would have become lost in the struggle over your refusal to use the toilet, what your mother called your stubbornness." He acknowledged that he could see how lost he must have felt. I proposed that as the issue got shifted to a battle over control, he would not have been able to reconnect with the friendly, well-trained boy mother had viewed him to be, that he always wishes to think himself to be. He responded, "I see that, and it's helpful."

The following hour, he returned to his more usual state of dissatisfaction. The progress he said had come from me. I expected it to come from him, and he couldn't produce it. We reviewed his hearing aggravation in my voice when he had blocked and been unproductive. I asked him about my sense yesterday that he had been unusually open to my suggestions. He then recalled that he didn't automatically pay my bill to get rid of it as always before, but actually looked at it. I asked if touching and looking at my bill had been like the danger of touching and looking at a toilet. He exclaimed, "Of course—I couldn't ever touch it—even at home, if I sat on the seat, I held my buttocks from touching."

"I am back from a triumphant visit to the stadium," was Mr. N's introduction to the next session. He had been able to urinate in a stadium men's room for the first time. He thought about hiding and privacy, shame and fear. He had appreciated my suggestion that his mother had become confused by his stubbornness and hadn't understood his fear. All she saw was he had lost his training. I suggested that his being trained so early had been largely by ritual rather than being agreed on and worked out by speech, that when he lost the ritual, he may have lost an easy flow into speech. He reflected for a moment and noted the similarity to his shifting from more fluid to more labored speech if any tension mounts between us. I added that if speech became an accusation about his stubbornness then the dialogue between him and his mother would have been further derailed, forcing him back into ritual. He said, like the ritual of having his bowel movements under the piano. He must have been trying to show her he was afraid, but he couldn't tell her. A silence followed during which I wondered about that puzzling memory. To my surprise and delight, he broke the silence by asking, "Why under the piano?" I noted with a chuckle that he was venturing to raise an "analytic question" on his own. With unusual vigor he responded, "That's where mother and Jay would sit and play together. Maybe I had been saying, Shit on you, if you two play together and leave me out?" Then, sadly, he reflected that he'd have been better off if he had learned to play the piano, too.

Freddy made his appearance early in the analysis in the first instance of an explicit, unguarded feeling of sadness by Mr. N. With a flow of tears, he had described his feelings of loss when he was 13 and Freddy died. Freddy would be brought up from time to time whenever either of us wanted to refer to Mr. N's capacity for positive affection or to admire liveliness. At times Freddy's appearance in a dream seemed to be an attempt to cheer himself up and soothe away his anxiety and depression. In another dream, Freddy was portrayed as in danger from snakes as he romped in the yard. I suggested that Mr. N may have enjoyed similar romping but had become frightened. He quickly assured me that although he enormously enjoyed watching Freddy, he could not imagine himself ever doing that because his mother very sensibly always made him wear shoes. The distance between Freddy and a playful image of himself could not be bridged until much further exploration of Mr. N's fears and resentments. After his fourth year of treatment, Mr. N married an attractive intelligent young woman, and gradually the work with each model scene came together. He could imagine that before the traumas of his third year, he might have been more like Freddy "frisking about, greeting everyone with eagerness, and showing his happiness with undisguised joy."

Toward the end of his therapy, now married and less entwined with his parents, Mr. N had a dream about war, fear, and snakes—elements we both regarded as pointing to his fear of a recurrence of eruptions of rage in response to humiliation. I suggested he was afraid that without the treatment, he might have trouble controlling the snake of his temper, the potential for engaging in holy wars of self-righteous vengeance. I added that he might believe he couldn't experience the full range of his emotions, including anger, without fearing to be so full of resentment and vengeance as to destroy the more Freddy-like self he had discovered. He responded, "To be able to experience disappointment and anger, particularly with my mother, and not have it interfere with being the kind of person I want to be, is to accept my mother as she wants to be and not have it distract me from the approach I want to take. It's a continuing struggle, and it's very helpful to have the perspective I've gained."

ENACTMENTS

For a long time, analytic theoreticians believed that the only way to gain the information needed for interpretation was from the spoken word delivered as free association. Action, broadly defined as any nonverbal form of communication, was regarded as a dilution, a resistance, and a defense against the needed verbal associations. Acting in or acting out were terms used to describe a patient's placing of the conflict outside of interpretable verbal associations and thereby lessening the potential for effective interpretation and change. The presumed opposition between actions and verbalizations has been revised for several reasons. Speech and gesture and other nonverbal communications are all actions. Rather than communication taking either verbal or nonverbal forms, according to which, if one is present the other is not, verbal and nonverbal actions are parallel processes that are continuously present. An additional important reason is that successful exploratory therapy requires sensing into the messages contained in both verbal and enactive forms. Returning to the mind as theater analogy, if an actor is telling a woman how deeply smitten he is with her, the audience will be far more convinced if his body is sensed to be prepared to mold into an embrace and his eyes and ears are resonant with hers. The background to this observation is that many aspects of our being are expressed via procedural memories that bear the mark of past experience. These procedural memories prime us to send and respond to messages in nonverbal forms. The nonverbal body forms are roles or patterned ways of being with others that come as automatically as a boxer assuming a boxing stance when his sparring partner does.

Of course, in therapy, the verbal–nonverbal action parallel lines of communication are often subtle. A patient described a number of successes. His tone was sincere, and he offered details to support his claims. At first, I was pleased to hear about the positive occurrences. Gradually I found myself, largely my body posture, tense rather than relaxed. I noticed that his partially visible hand was stroking his leg in a self-soothing gesture. His words were telling one story while his hand and body tension were telling another, and I was receiving both. Consciously I was attending the verbal story with the linear word organized part of my brain; unconsciously I was responding to cueing from an enacted story of tension. I asked the patient if, despite his successes, he might be feeling tense. He looked puzzled, and I asked him to notice his hand, suggesting he might be soothing his tension. Feeling criticized, he exclaimed, "What's wrong with that?" I said, "Nothing is wrong with soothing yourself if it helps to reduce your tension. The problem I see is that if you are tense and aren't letting yourself be aware of it, we can't discover what might be troubling you, especially at a time when you are reporting accomplishments you have worked hard to bring about." "Oh," he answered, "now that you mention it, I remember wondering if I should bring up the successes. I was worried you'd think I was just bragging, puffing up, and you would feel you had to cut me down to size."

At this point, after his metaphoric statement, "cut me down to size," the patient and I both recalled a model scene with which we had often worked. When he would tell his mother about a good grade, his father would say, "That boy is getting too big for his britches; he's not as smart as he thinks he is." Paradoxically, in a fashion we did enact a "put down." When I asked him about his tension, I did burst the bubble of his effort to remain upbeat. Further, he took my reference to his self-soothing as a criticism not unlike his father's perceived attacks on his manhood. This was a specific enactment about his masculinity within an enactment about "bragging." For the moment I chose to pass over the masculinity issue to try to understand the more immediate and accessible meaning of the tension signaled by his fear of being cut down for bragging.

Enactments once recognized become valuable sources of information. Even when therapists accepted their value for exploration, enactments were often regarded as failures on the part of the therapist to remain outside the immediacy of the problems, able to be focused only on the patient, either empathically or as an observer. To find themselves enmeshed in an enactment has meant to therapists that they were involved in a countertransference problem. In a contemporary perspective, the subtleties of communication during intensive therapy conducted with a spirit of inquiry allow enactments to be viewed as far more enhancing. Each partner in the dyad brings to his or her exchanges a form of nonverbal communication that contributes to each being pulled into an enactment unaware of the enmeshing cueing and responding. Each member of the dyad may unknowingly be exerting a pull on the other to engage in a particular role that has historical significance for him. Each member of the dyad may unknowingly be more or less open or susceptible to assume a role into which he is being unconsciously cued. Residues of traumatic lived experiences result in patients cueing their therapists into assuming interactive roles such as dominator–submitter, victimizer–victim, omnipotent–powerless, intimidator–fearful, seducer–seduced, abandoner–abandoned, intruder–invaded. Alternatively, therapists can unwittingly cue patients toward roles of overcompliance, rebelliousness, dependence, or neediness.

Enactments exert a paradoxical effect on therapists doing intensive exploration. If therapists are too ritualized in their approach, they may strenuously resist the experience of being drawn into a role-responsive stance. They then sacrifice a valuable source of information. Moreover, the needed subjectivity of each member of the dyad is replaced by an illusion that the therapist is solely an objective observer and interpreter of the patient's psyche. The paradox is that for a therapist to persist in illusory objectivity constitutes another form of enactment. Therapists who hypervigilantly resist nonverbal enactment engagements produce an enactment in which suspicion prevails.

For most of the history of psychoanalysis, communication through enactment rather than words has been believed to be a threat to the treatment. This view of threat may have prevailed because the principles of technique needed to seize the opportunity inherent in the enacted mode of communication had not yet been formulated. In their aggregate, the principles of technique presented in each chapter of this work constitute an approach that retains the value of exploring the verbal–affective message and gives comparable status to exploring the nonverbal implicit enactive–affective message.

Although particularly suited for bringing enactive communication to the foreground, the construction of model scenes facilitates an inquiry into both symptoms and memories and into current enactments. Mr. N's memory of defecating under the piano was an enactment of his hostility toward his mother and his envy of his brother. The nonverbal experience that this memory invoked in me was that of puzzled wonderment about its meaning, not an enactment of the roles of his mother and him. The model scene was a straightforward collaboration employing symbolic associations to augment the latent motives behind the scene. Looking at the therapeutic process more broadly, Mr. N's persistent withholding, long and disconnecting silences, and general attacking obstinacy evoked impatient frustration and irritability that I had to let myself experience, recognize, and struggle to contain within workable limits. We might speak of this interplay between us as one long nonverbal enactment. A portion of the model scene that we shared and utilized for understanding repeatedly was the analogy to his angry resistant push–pull struggle with his mother on a long variety of issues between us. A portion of the model scene I silently kept in mind for a long time was a general battle over toilet training with intense shaming and difficulty explaining intense fearfulness. In the case example, I illustrated the explanatory value of the model scenes we developed late in the treatment. Only then were the conditions right for cocreating a model scene suggested by dreams and associations that in greater detail centered on his brother's kidney disease and specific issues of bowel regulation that had persisted for years—as had our enacted struggles with retention, constriction, and fear.

CASE EXAMPLE

Three episodes from the treatment of Sister Mary (Lichtenberg, 2000), a middle-aged parochial school teacher, illustrate model scenes that helped to unravel the meanings of enactments. Sister Mary began her exploratory therapy raging at me with a totally unexpected outpouring of invective. Although she later explained that her previous therapist had explained the failure of their work as due to her inability or unwillingness to "express" her anger, the hatred she generated seemed quite genuine. Sister Mary did hate a lot of people and could be sadistic to them. I endured her attacks as tolerantly as I could. I responded to any opening that she offered to comment on her feelings or the narrative she was relating. To my surprise, she informed me that she experienced me as treating her sadistically. I was, she said, continuously punishing her with silence. Because attacks and accusations dominated her communications, her assuming that we were locked in roles of mutual antagonism was not surprising. What was surprising was the role assigned to me of punishing her with "the silent treatment," an accusation she might make within moments after I had spoken in what I thought was a nonhostile voice. She waved aside the contradiction, leading me to view the enactment as meaning that, whether or not I spoke, she might experience herself as being punished at times that seemed too random for me to relate to either her associations or my feelings or responses.

On one occasion, she described her indignation at a pupil who had complained to the pupil's mother about Sister Mary's treatment of her. Sister Mary announced that she had tried to help the child but would do so no more. I asked spontaneously, "Will you punish her with the silent treatment?" She answered, "Yes, like my mother did." This opened the way to our "constructing" a model scene of the patient's mother who, whenever irked by anything, singled out one of the children and in a loud, haughty stage whisper said to the others, "Don't talk to her, we ignore her." Once made into a pariah, the child had no appeal until the sentence was lifted at an unpredictable time. I could not predict the occasions when Sister Mary would regard herself to be the victim of my silent ostracism, but when she entered my office, her nose in the air in an attitude of unchallengeable hauteur, I knew I was to be the victim of her retaliation. The memory scenes from childhood and the current enactments with shifting punisher–pariah roles permitted us to construct a model scene of our engagements that facilitated moments of sharing an appreciation of who and what we could be locked into with each other.

Another enactment occurred in the form of a dramatic exchange between us. Only later as a memory scene came into focus were we able to cocreate a model scene. Sister Mary was advisor to a young adult who was considering joining their order. The young woman, Grace, became very attached and dependent. With a mixture of defiance and shame, Sister Mary revealed that they embraced often and fondled one another. Included in my attempts to understand and interpret Sister Mary's motivation were expressions of my concern about appearances and exposure. Sister Mary was generally so rebellious about rules that my concerns about risk went unappreciated and unheeded. She reported in a glow that she had had a wonderful weekend. Grace had come and agreed to stay over. They had undressed and fondled all over and satisfied themselves lovingly. In a voice that revealed my mixture of disapproval, concern, and alarm, I said she was involving herself sexually against her own commitments as a spiritual advisor. Even more of a problem, she was sexually enticing a young woman who had placed her trust in her. She became outraged, telling me that everything I said was further proof of my dirty mind. She insisted that their embracing was an expression of love. It provided her with a badly needed affirmation that she was worthy of love, and that her large body, so deprecated by her mother, was being appreciated by another woman. She roared, "This was love, not sex!" Without reflection, I roared back, "When you and another person get in bed naked and masturbate one another that is sex! Whatever else is involved, it is sex!" A silence followed that seemed both an expression of exhaustion after the intensity of emotion, but also to involve reflection on both our parts as we regained our composure (self-righted).

What followed was unexpected. Sister Mary explained to Grace that they could not continue. It was not good for either. Grace needed to look elsewhere for a loving relationship (which she subsequently did). I remained puzzled by Sister Mary's compliance because it was so divergent from her usual overt or covert rejection of authority. Later as we were considering her relations with men, she described an episode from her early teen years. A neighborhood boy and she had formed a crush on one another and, somewhat flamboyantly, were publicly affectionate. Word of their flirtation got back to her parents. One morning before going to work, her father yanked her out of bed, sat her down in the kitchen, told her what he had heard, and called her a little whore. He raised his hand in a gesture he called the "right hand of the law" and forbade her to have anything further to do with the boy. Terrified and cowed, she agreed. She could defy her mother, find all kinds of creative ways to get around her, but not her father. She was genuinely fond of her father, whose good opinion of her she desperately wanted to retain and whose wrath she genuinely feared. Using our interchange about Grace and the memory of her father's emotion-laden insistence, we could understand her acceptance of my "eruption" (a disciplined spontaneous engagement, see chapter 9). Further we could begin to recognize that whether she responded to rules and prohibitions with defiance or acceptance was determined by her perception of the authority as being either like her mother or her father. Sister Mary was now willing to look more deeply into her techniques of disciplining children. She started to appreciate the wounding effect of her silent ostracism, and the panic she inspired by her austere "right hand of the law" terrorizing.

The first enactment was triggered by Sister Mary's idiosyncratic response to my more-or-less ordinary silence. The second enactment arose from my response to her dangerous sexual behavior. The model scenes that helped to illuminate the source of the enactment came from her past experiences. The enactment I now describe arose largely from my blindness to my own behavior and the explanatory model scene from my own life experience.

The ups and downs of Sister Mary's provocative behavior with authorities led the leaders of her order to question the efficacy of the treatment and their financial support. Her anger was now shifted off of me and directed to those who threatened her as she tenaciously held to her need and desire to continue. I helped by arranging a consultation with the psychiatric advisor to the diocese. He reported that she was making significant progress and advised that her outpatient treatment, while she served a professional function, was much less expensive than a long or repeated short hospitalizations. Continued support was authorized, and Sister Mary now redirected her belligerence to me. I dealt with the attacks and devaluing much as I had before, trying to recognize the source in any occurrence between us or any carryover from the many exigencies of her daily life.

In the past, this approach had been both stabilizing and effective in adding to our understanding, but now progress was stalled. The devaluing intensified, and I was at a loss to relate it to anything I was doing. Sister Mary also became increasingly desperate and arranged for a consultation with the referring therapist. She returned saying he reassured her that of course her attacks bothered me. This comment opened my eyes to my contribution to our enactment. It was not what I was doing that had us at an impasse; it was what I was not doing. I was not letting her know that I was really troubled by the things she told me I was doing wrong. I was depriving her of the satisfaction of knowing that her attacks got through my professional armor and caused a sting. In the beginning of the treatment, by her own acknowledgment, my "not taking it personally" had been central to her feeling safe. Now she wanted me to take it personally. She had to have me take it personally. Unless I was distressed, she couldn't believe I knew that attacks on her she had told me about really hurt her. Looking inward, I realized that I was reliving a response from childhood when an intimate member of my family had under the pressure of the terrible pain of illness become angry and critical, and I had developed the strategy of absorbing the attacks with minimal emotional responses of retaliation while discounting much of the exaggeration in the content. This ability to deflect attacks without impairing my attention, what might be called becoming thick-skinned, had been useful in my early work with Sister Mary but had now become a distinct constraint on our progress. With the memory scene from my childhood available to me, I began to build a model scene of the meaning to us of my withholding from her the recognition of the power of her protests not just to alert me to her distress, but to wound, to get under my skin. We could examine how I was contributing to her increasingly desperate need to be heard and how this led her to increase the amplitude of her attacks. From the work with the model scene informing each of our contributions, Sister Mary came to recognize how desperately she needed the empowering quality of anger to convey and cope with her lifelong feelings of shame and powerlessness, and I learned the great significance of knowing and acknowledging an ouch!

In chapter 6, I presented a reconsideration of "transference"; in this chapter, a contemporary understanding of "enactments." In chapter 8, I will consider a third mainstay of psychoanalytic theory—the concept of defense. I will describe guidelines for therapists to recognize, understand, and explore a wide range of aversive responses that patients employ.

CHAPTER 8

HOW TO RESPOND TO A MESSAGE THAT INDICATES THERE IS SOMETHING A PATIENT DOESN'T WANT HIMSELF, HIS THERAPIST, OR BOTH TO KNOW

THROUGHOUT THE PERIOD IN WHICH EGO PSYCHOLOGY dominated the approach to analytic therapy, defense interpretation occupied a privileged position. Associations were conceptualized as layered in such a manner that troubling memories, thoughts, motives, and values were sequestered behind a wall of resistances, defense mechanisms, and behaviors. Analysts had first to recognize the defensive activity, then interpret it, and then seek to interpret the content (unconscious fantasy) sequestered "behind" it. My view is that aversive motives (resistance, reluctance, and defensiveness) are a communicative expression to be explored like any other message. Only when antagonism or withdrawal in any of their manifestations are perceived to be dominant in the foreground do they receive our primary focus. The guiding principle is that privilege is granted to whatever motivation the therapist considers to be dominant. Carrying this guideline further, we are alert to those negative emotions that trigger or are triggered by an aversive response: anger, rage, fear, panic, shame, embarrassment, humiliation, sadness, depression.

Before discussing the view I hold, let us consider this issue by examining aversive motives (or defensive operations) in the example of Sister Mary in chapter 7. Manifestly, Sister Mary poured out venom toward me and others from the first day of treatment. As long as her expressions of antagonism filled the stage, she could keep from revealing to herself and to me her extreme vulnerability to hurt feelings and devaluation. That is, she could bury her painful sense of shame under her bluster and defiance. By maintaining a constant and replenished list of enemies, mostly women, she could hide from herself and others tender feelings she was certain would not be returned. She maintained a private life of prayer shared with one spiritual advisor who had a sustaining faith in her. A loving tender God the Father replaced her father who, although loving to her, also terrified her.

Toward the end of her lengthy treatment, she was ranting to a friend about her hatred for the modern art in my office when the friend asked her if she ever looked at it. Startled, she admitted that she hadn't and determined on a parting present for me. She arranged for an artist to make a paper leaf book with cartoonlike drawings of artworks. The text told how all along she had hated my modern art until finally she realized that I had helped her to broaden her perspective and become open to appreciation and affection. Looking back, I would say Sister Mary did not want to know the deep-seated sense of shame she felt about her body, her sexuality, her sadism, and her terrible sense of being humiliated and devalued, especially by her mother. Equally, she did not want me to know about her tender feelings for fear of my failure to recognize, accept, and appreciate them. She also did not want either of us to know that a mutual fondness had developed despite her continuing belligerence.

The dramatic discoveries of psychoanalysis that captured the imagination of the world were couched in such evocative metaphors as an archeologist searching for the buried truths of the past or a surgeon's careful dissection and removal of a pathological growth. Both metaphors suggested a barrier, the accretions of later civilizations or the body surface covering something that needed to be found and released. The something that needed to be found and freed changed from strangulated affect to repressed memories to manifestations of drive distortion, especially infantile fantasy. The method of discovery and release was regarded as interpretation, first of the barrier (unconscious defenses), and then the fantasy of which a psychoneurotic system was a symbolic expression. The finding of Freud that shook the Victorian world was that children, even infants, had sexual desires. The study of psychosexual development, of oral, anal, phallic, and oedipal stages, of the fantasies of each and their language of symbolism expressed in dreams, symptoms, and slips of the tongue, presented analysts with a vision of an unknown world. Analysts thereby could believe they were endowed with the equivalent of x-ray vision that allowed them to penetrate the surface barriers and identify a significant oral, anal, or oedipal symbolic fantasy. Analysts discovered that informing patients of the complexes they "knew" were hidden frequently led only to an intellectual response. To gain the desired therapeutic result, analytic theoreticians concluded that the barrier itself had to be brought into consciousness through the interpretation of the patient's use of defenses such as repression, isolation, and denial. Thus, the privileged position of defense interpretation.

A contrast between the traditional approach and the approach I recommend can be seen in a therapist's (Ann) tracking of aversive responses during a therapy session with T, a 28-year-old graduate student. During several prior sessions T had mentioned that he might not be able to remain in therapy because of the cost.

PATIENT: I've had financial trouble this week. My air-conditioner broke, and it cost me $1000.
ANALYST: Oh no! [Ann's exclamation was emitted spontaneously in response to what T had told her and the concern for the therapy it had triggered in her, not, she quickly realized, in response to T's affect, which was unemotional, matter-of-fact reporting.]

PATIENT: [after a brief silence] It's OK because I know the repairman, and he'll get it fixed. . . . I had put away enough money for a breakdown, but I didn't think I'd be hit with that big an expense.
ANALYST: [realizing her confusion about T's affect] How do you feel about it?

PATIENT: Sad . . . and I can't make plans yet for how Diane (his

fiancée) and I are going to afford next year when she starts law school because her parents haven't come forward yet with what they will contribute.
ANALYST: You're uncomfortable with the lack of planning.

PATIENT: And having to be dependent. That's worse. . . . It's important to be independent. Diane's parents talk about all the self-sacrifice they go through, and I don't want to hear it. My family gave us kids a lot, but they don't talk about it. When I was a kid I wanted to put on a puppet show with my best friend and charge admission. My dad loaned us the money to make the stage and charged us interest on the loan. I learned that if you borrow money, it costs you, but if you save money, you make money.
ANALYST: So to be independent is very important.

PATIENT: Independence means freedom. That's why after my long bout with mono I went on a tough wilderness survival program. When you are all alone in the wilderness, you learn responsibility—how to deal with life-and-death decisions. That experience made me different from other people. Remember I told you the other grad students were panicking about the oral exam. Well, I didn't feel nervous. I was eager, not nervous.
ANALYST: So your wilderness survival experience gave you a unique perspective. When you've dealt with life-or-death decisions, you know what real nervousness is.

PATIENT: Yes . . . [Laughing] Maybe I can work on money next. The situation with Diane and her parents doesn't have to make me nervous. . . . Oh, I asked my mom about my memory of the first house we lived in before my sister was born, and Mom said I had it right. She said I played a lot by myself, that I was either close to her or off alone. In nursery school, the teacher told Mom I wanted to sit on her lap all the time and that maybe I needed more attention. Mom said she laughed and told her, "Why, he sits on my lap half the time, so I don't think so."
ANALYST: What do you think?

PATIENT: I don't know. My mom says I got lots of attention, so maybe I wanted it in school, too.
ANALYST: Yes, that could be . . . or maybe it didn't feel enough . . . maybe you felt that you needed to be held a lot.

PATIENT: That reminds me how I got teased when I was little and pleaded with Mom to hold my hand or pick me up. I was sensitive about it—embarrassed when they'd say, "Don't you ever get enough!"

The exchange between T and the therapist can be viewed either from a perspective that asks what defenses or resistances require interpretation or from one that asks, in general, what experiences need to be understood, and in particular what aversive experiences need to be tracked and explored. I examine two segments of the session from each perspective.

In the opening dialogue, T's lack of emotion can be regarded as his unconscious use of the defense mechanism of isolation of affect. He has separated his thoughts from his feelings. From this perspective, the therapist's task is to draw the patient's attention to the employment of this mechanism, help him to recognize that he has a need to protect himself from the dystonic affect of anxiety, and therefore promote entry into consciousness of the warded-off affect. Three benefits would be expected to derive from this approach. First, the patient would repair the disunity of thought and feeling. Second, he would learn that when threatened by anxiety, he resorts unconsciously to this particular mechanism to prevent experiencing an affect frightening to him as a child but tolerable to him as an adult. Third, the anxiety once brought into awareness might be related by interpretation to an unconscious fantasy such as his dependant desire for oral gratification. This fantasy in turn might be viewed as a regressive defense against his oedipal possessiveness of his mother. In this perspective, the therapist's alarm would be regarded as a countertransference response to her fear of losing the patient with whatever anal (money) or oedipal desire it stirred in her.

Still from the perspective of giving primacy to a focus on defense, the therapist's anxiety could be regarded as the result of a projective identification in which T had projected his abandonment dread into her, causing her, not him, to take alarm at the threat of a rupture. The buildup of threats to continuing before the session would be an enactment that was a component of the defensive process. The advantage to the therapist adopting this view is that she could free herself of the unconscious impediment to her neutral position as observer and interpret what was taking place in their relationship.

Alternatively, from a perspective of inquiry into T's experience, the therapist would first be drawn to recognize what was happening at the junction of their interplay. She would examine her own spontaneous exclamation and restore (self-regulate) her affect state. Her self-righting did occur rapidly. She was then able to refocus on T's message-as-delivered and to recognize the discrepancy between his content and the expected affect of concern. The discrepancy then became a subject for exploration. She could surmise that anxiety probably was aversive to him, but her interest turned to the nature of his experience from his point of view. She could not glean his view from their initial colloquy. Her interest in his affect, demonstrated by her question about his feeling and her open-minded listening stance, allowed her to follow the initial meanings of his assertions about independence and the training he received in financial management. Now Ann could form a working hypothesis. From T's point of view, he was experiencing a businesslike acceptance of the vagaries of equipment costs and was proud to demonstrate to her and to himself that he had learned this "independent" approach to money management. The meaning from his standpoint, a meaning not in full awareness but experientially available, is that he is demonstrating his success as a planner. At that moment he is not experiencing himself as having isolated anxiousness, as an observer might surmise. The motivation he could sense to be dominant at that moment was based on his exploratory–assertive attempt to achieve efficiency and competence in planning for reversals. He derived pride from doing so. In his experience his affect and content were well coordinated. I believe this recognition of his perspective by the therapist facilitated T's later in the session's playful acknowledgment, "Maybe I can work on money next," establishing an opening to a later inquiry.

The second episode in the session deals with another source of emotion—T's taking oral exams in graduate school. He states that unlike other students who were nervous, he was eager. From the standpoint of a focus on defense, the therapist could assume T was using denial to cover his fear. She could buttress this assumption by his association that after a long, debilitating illness he had resorted to a denial-in-action by volunteering for survival training. She would then have drawn his attention to the conflict between his wanting to be independent and fearless and his natural concerns about health and exams. He keeps these concerns out of awareness by denying them. In fact, the therapist did deal directly with disavowal at the end of the session when she suggested to T that in contradistinction to his accepting his mother's version, he may have felt that his mother's holding was not sufficient.

From the standpoint of his perspective, T was emphasizing to Ann and to himself the dramatic lengths to which he had gone to experience himself prepared, even eager, to face dangerous situations on his own. Guided by this perception of him, Ann acknowledged to him that she had heard the full significance to him of the mastery experience in the wilderness, his life-or-death perspective. In my view, the empathic understanding and responsiveness conveyed by this acknowledgment contributed to T's openness to two subsequent associations. First, he returned to the theme of the early part of the session and, comforting himself with humor, he admitted to nervousness about money. Second, he began the key associations to his childhood dependent attachment struggle with his mother. As he spoke about this important embarrassing memory, he approached the subject through a series of distancing rhetorical forms: "Oh, by the way, it just occurred to me"; "I'm just reporting what others—mother, the nursery teacher—have said"; and the conjectural use of "maybe."

The therapist now had a choice. She could either describe the use of the distancing rhetorical forms to T or disregard their effect for the present. The first path could lead into a productive exploration of defensive aspects of word use in communication and its place in an aversive motivation. The goal would be to open the way to more vivid affective renderings of experience. I would recommend this path if the distancing rhetoric were rigidly maintained as a self-protective means. The second path, which Ann followed, is more direct and economical. From the relative openness that had emerged, she sensed that T would be able to join her in exploring his attachment struggle without feeling overwhelmed by shame or forced into compliance. She knew she would examine the sequence of subsequent exchanges to evaluate the effect of her bypassing the defensive rhetoric and intervening more directly. Ann first asked T to give his thoughts and then offered him her perception of his childhood needs and the feeling state that accompanied it: "Maybe it didn't feel enough." After Ann's gentle pushing aside of his aversive hiding behind his mother's account, T described his sensitivity and embarrassment in response to the family teasing.

Tracking T's experience in the way Ann did would open the path into two lines of inquiry. The first would be his pride–shame conflict about money, which he had flagged. The second would be the enactment of his threats to interrupt the therapy and the (possible? probable?) link to a desire to climb into Ann's lap and be held very tight. Shame would again present a strong trigger of aversiveness that Ann would have to help him experience and feel safe to expose to her and to himself.

The goal Ann followed was to help T and herself to understand the meanings of their enactment about continuing the therapy. Ann uses T's memories to help explore T's here-and-now motivations. This reverses the archeological and surgical metaphors to reveal the "truth" of the past and free the patient from infantile distortion. Rather than using the symptoms, associations, and dreams of the present to discover or uncover the past, we use knowledge of the past to help explore and understand the present. Although we can never fully understand the here and now of patients and ourselves without an appreciation of the past, our goal in exploratory therapies is to open the present to understanding and change.

So what do we reconceptualize and what do we retain? To reconfigure what defense or resistance means, the broadest view is that the concept refers to a person having an experience of something undesired or undesirable. Troubling past experiences and/or analogous troubling present experiences can be barred from fully or partially coming into awareness. Likewise, the implications or meanings of troubling experience may be treated defensively as without significance. An example that harkens back to Freud's early descriptions of repression comes from Nancy (chapters 5 and 6), about whom I say more now.

Nancy reported that she was upset about not being able to find a bag in which she kept a number of pieces of jewelry. She was moving out of her house to allow for renovations, and as she packed she went to where the jewelry bag was and it was gone. She searched everywhere to no avail. The only thing she could think of was that she had given a number of discarded items to Goodwill. Had the bag gotten mixed in? She hated to lose the jewelry but equally bad was the feeling of being so foolish. I commented that the feeling of being foolish brought back many memories of being teased and humiliated. She agreed and said she has been beating on herself enough but can't get over not taking care of these valued pieces. I asked her to tell me what was in the bag. The most valuable was a small but fine diamond that had belonged to her mother's mother and was given to her mother's older sister. Childless, the sister left it to Nancy's mother to be given to a female descendant. Nancy (also childless) had never worn it. The setting was old-fashioned and unattractive. Nancy had taken it to a jeweler to have it made into a necklace. This jeweler refused, saying diamonds put in necklaces are too easily lost. Frustrated Nancy gave up for now, thinking later she'd change the setting for a ring. She couldn't wear it around any of her cousins without stirring their resentment that she had it. A ruby pin and earrings had been given to her by an aunt who just died and whose bequest was paying for Nancy's house renovations. Before her death, the aunt had asked each niece to select a piece of jewelry. One cousin and a sister-in-law used the opportunity to attack Nancy for having her aunt's financial manager pay Nancy's travel expenses to make regular planned visits to spend time with her aunt. Nancy had decided she wanted to help relieve her aunt's loneliness—no one else visited regularly—but to travel so far would seriously drain her limited resources. So she and the financial manager made the arrangement that the estate (a large one) would pay. I asked Nancy for the numbers, and the loss to the others in their inheritance from the outlay to Nancy was trivial. Nonetheless, they were outraged and Nancy had to hold on to her own perspective to keep from getting involved in a nasty fight. Several of the other jewelry pieces had similar stories of jealousy, competitiveness, and disappointments—a meaning I noted to her. As the session ended, Nancy added that while the objects had some monetary value and many connections to her family, they were not the jewelry she ever wore or really liked.

The next session, Nancy said the mystery is solved. After our last session, she was walking by the table on which she had put the sack of items for Goodwill. She suddenly had an image of the sack and sticking out at the bottom was a red color—the bag with the jewelry. She had meant to check it out but didn't, and when she bundled it all up she must have included it. We then discussed her struggle to free herself from the entanglements with her family to be fully able to enjoy the life of productivity and excellent relations she had constructed for herself. Her aunt's death, the inheritance after years and years of promise, had stirred up again the family animosity toward her and her shame at being an outsider, the one whose father wasn't a success. The jewelry evoked mother's discontents—another "inheritance" from mother's rich family. Nancy concluded that she was unconsciously trying to divest herself of the aversive memories of her past. Doing so in this way, however, brought back her feelings of being a "doofus" and that hurt. She said she could get over that now without falling into a depression. She ended the session saying she hoped whoever got the sack would find the pieces and be able to enjoy them in a way she never could.

I return to the task of reconceptualizing defense and resistance as one of many communicative messages by moving from the narrowly specific clinical story of missing jewelry to the broad conception of systems of motivation. In my view, each human cocreates with those in his or her intersubjective environment a unique system of responding to whatever is found to be aversive. A system organized in response to the need to react to whatever is experienced as aversive takes its place along with systems organized to respond to a need for physiological requirements, attachment and affiliative connection and security, exploring and asserting preferences, and seeking sensual pleasure and sexual excitement. Each system cocreates in conjunction with the facilitating or interfering influence of the environment. Each system (the child's motivational systems and the caregiver–child intersubjective system) self-organizes, self-stabilizes, exists in dialectic tension with other systems and with different tendencies within the system, and, in the course of development, undergoes hierarchical rearrangement. Responses to aversion organize around two opposite innate tendencies: the inclination to be antagonistic or oppositional and the inclination to withdraw. Anger in all its manifestations is the affective trigger for antagonism. Fear, sadness, shame, humiliation, and embarrassment are common triggers for withdrawal.

The aversive system has a unique optimal developmental trajectory. Being able to organize and regulate nutrient intake, elimination, sleep, attachment connectedness, exploration, and sensual pleasure in the first year are quintessential tasks of infant–caregiver interchanges. An infant's development is placed at a decided disadvantage, however, if he or she is forced to consolidate patterns of antagonism as in anxious–resistant attachment or withdrawal as in avoidant attachment or, worse yet, to try to work out how to be with a primary caregiver by vacillating between angry approach and fearful pulling back into a chaotic state of disorganization or disorientation. Thus in the first year optimal organization of the aversive system is to cocreate with the caregiver a set of increasingly clear signals of distress or negative preferences that a caregiver can recognize and respond to. The function of the aversive system to provide recognizable signals continues throughout life so that we can tell ourselves and others what we don't like or want, what upsets or distresses us. By the second year, optimal development of the aversive system moves from primarily indications of communicative signals to consolidating the ability to engage in controversy, in struggles over opposing agendas with caregivers. This begins two lifelong tasks. The first is to be able to engage in disagreements, assert one's position, assert power when needed, retain a sense of autonomy, and enjoy victory or defeat without sacrificing the ability to restore a needed attachment. The second task is to appraise danger and develop an adaptive flexible variety of means to retreat from its immediate effect and seek safety.

Defenses and resistance are best seen in this broader context of an aversive motivational system of antagonistic and withdrawal (fight–flight) response patterns. This broad sweep omits the crucial factor of how antagonism and withdrawal are dealt with once symbolic language, imagery, and play reorder the child's affective interactive life. Toward the end of a lengthy treatment, George, describing something he had learned about himself, said, "When I really want something, I am apt to keep it from myself, but when I let myself know, I still pull back from asserting my desire because I have been so certain my wish will be rejected and I will be called selfish for asking. So I go along with what others want me to do, and then my desire and frustration goes underground and bubbles up as irritation and resentment. Then I try to soothe myself with food, look for a woman to have sex with to calm me down, or go off into fantasy. By then I've lost touch with my original desire. Only now with what we've learned have I been able to find it again."

George has learned to give words to his struggles with his desires and to be reflectively aware of his mode of thinking, feeling, and behaving. He places the other as rejecting and shaming and sees his withdrawal into compliance as an understandable consequence. He uses logical syntactic speech and also metaphoric speech (underground and bubbles up). His speech indicates his secure attachment to his therapist in that it is collaborative, clear, logical, affective, and succinct. Thus, for an adult in an exploratory therapy, speech and enactment (dyadic communication) becomes the vehicle for the expression of aversiveness, and therefore for its interpretation.

In any given session, we can observe the ebb and flow of aversiveness. In the example just given, the patient had raised both desire and source of aversiveness into awareness, giving him the opportunity to risk asserting his wish or plan or goal rather than automatically adopting a strategy of compliance with all its consequences. In the example of Nancy and the lost jewelry, she was unaware of how the objects had come to be symbolic of her resentment for family members' hurtful treatment of her. She was caught between her negative feelings about individual family members (largely anxious–resistant attachments) and a positive orientation toward family loyalty (an affiliative motive).

The example of Sister Mary introduces recognition of another factor in understanding defense and resistance. I have said aversive motivations are a communicative expression to be explored like any other. As with any other verbal and nonverbal communication or enactment, we focus on patients' withdrawing, fending off, provoking, denying, and obfuscating from the point of view of what the patient experiences. Only when a patient like Nancy and George can bring into awareness aversiveness as a subjective experience in an intersubjective context can therapist and patient ascertain the patient's motives as he or she construes them. The form of speech tells part of the aversive story, the content another part, and the state of the ambiance prevailing in the session still another. When the ambiance is animated but not overwhelmed by aversive affects, the potentiality of empathic listening, introspection, and reflective thinking allow for the understanding and interpreting of the contradictory desires, goals, and values presented. When aversive affects are intense and dominant, however, when a patient (or therapist, or both) are experiencing panic, severe depression, manic euphoria, searing shame, rage, a desire for vengeance, or have so blocked an affective response through dissociation and thought disorganization, a major constraint is placed on understanding at any level. The experience of constraint on understanding that was common in the treatment of Sister Mary and other borderline or dissociative patients is best characterized by an altered state of consciousness rather than defense. The knowledge George acquired of the meaning of his compliance and its bubbling-up consequences is not possible for a patient like Sister Mary in her raging state. In the altered states, enemies are enemies, consequences don't exist, effects are equated with intentions, symbolism becomes concrete without metaphoric nuance, every value is black or white, all or nothing, uncertainty vanishes, and all of life is condensed into the here and now. No time line exists and no reflection is possible. Only what serves the immediate aversive goal can be heard. Anything else constitutes a fresh assault on a fragile highly vulnerable sense of worth. The main problem in the treatment is not difficulty in processing aversiveness in the form of defense and resistance, but in gaining any regulation of aversive affective expression. Containment, being able to remain with, the patient and surviving as a caring professional are the main therapeutic challenges when faced with the constraints of here-and-now-limited consciousness.

Vestiges of unresolved trauma are common precipitants for a shift from higher-level consciousness to an altered state. The trauma may be an early serious disturbance in attachment experience, all manners of childhood and adult abuse, and shock experiences of accidents, catastrophes, and war. The title of this chapter, addressing how to respond to a message that indicates a patient doesn't want himself, the therapist, or both to know something, must be responded to differently depending on whether the patient is in a higher or altered state of consciousness. I offer two sessions from Nancy's treatment that reveal the struggle to work with her inclination to, as she often described it, fog out. Nancy's lapsing into a dissociative cognitive–affective blockage was especially likely to occur when the subject was about her older brother Matt's masturbation using her body. The traumatic effect was greatly intensified by her insecure attachment to her mother and her parents' denial of Matt's sexual abuse and frightening behavior. Alternatively, in the sessions when Nancy had self-righted from the dissociative pull, we could approach her aversiveness using an approach of symbolic language and imagistic language including dreams and then forge linkages using metaphor. With a reinstated higher level of consciousness and a collaborative communicative flow, we could explore her aversiveness to let herself and me know her deeper feelings and beliefs.

TUESDAY

Nancy began saying she had been able to make progress in a number of areas but nonetheless was feeling depressed. She added that if everything is in order, then she has no excuse to avoid problems she needs to deal with here. I responded that she was afraid that then she would feel she could or should talk with me about her sexual problems, as she had begun to do last week. She became physically limp and still and silent. I asked what she was experiencing.

> PATIENT: Fog. I feel I'm in a fog when I try to think about my sexual problems.

THERAPIST: Can you penetrate the fog to sense any of the factors? [I asked a question that was ambiguous, in that she could associate to the fog or to the sexual problems. She chose the latter.]

PATIENT: Being in my parents' bedroom, observing their sex and being confused. Getting enemas. The sexual activity with my brother. Being banished from my dad's lap. Being banished always from Mother. Never being able to snuggle or cuddle with her. [This had the quality of a recitation of lessons learned, but at the same time of lifting out of repression the results of a great deal of the prior therapeutic work that appears and disappears into the fog.]

PATIENT: It has all taken on the same character—of being bad, naughty. I got the enemas because I was bad—didn't go to the bathroom—and I was bad because the enemas gave me a lot of stimulation I liked. I was banished from Dad's lap over stimulation—my bad response. I couldn't be close to Mother because I was bad—it was put as dependence, but I don't know what it was. It wasn't that. [Her tone is a mixture of being troubled and guilty, of being both serious and facetious.] Everything sensual is all bad. Touching, masturbating in Dad's lap. All ends up being bad—wanting to stick like glue to mother. Not going to the bathroom. Teasing Matt, getting into sexual activities with him. All problems. My play with Margaret and the dolls doesn't seem so problematic—it was just 10-year-old stuff. What does it mean that I don't think it was problematic?
THERAPIST: Can you describe it?
[I answered a question with a question that is in fact a suggestion, the purpose being to fill the narrative envelope by moving from the too general to the specific, from the already said to experiences that had never been described.]

PATIENT: We were playing with our dolls, being mothers trying to breast-feed, although of course we didn't have breasts. We were holding the doll against our breasts and feeding it. Another day we were worried about breast cancer, checking out our flat

chests [laughing] at eight or nine. I don't remember much sensation. I was interested in my body. We had fantasies of being in love with movie stars—mine was Perry Mason, I was Della Street. We played doctor. One was sick, the other came to listen to the patient's chest and stomach. We had play stethoscopes. We were undressed partially. It had nothing to do with genitals. It all had to do with our nonexistent breasts [pause]. It was not dirty. It was clean. There were no secretions. With my brother, it was ejaculation that was sick, gross. As you said before, in the play with Margaret we were equals. My brother would rub against me. Against my leg, my stomach, until he had ejaculations. I felt very dirty and used.
[This added considerable richness of detail. It was stated with feeling but without a sense of becoming overwhelmed with revulsion, as in the past.]
THERAPIST: With your brother, you didn't have a sense of being appreciated for yourself but for the purpose you served?

PATIENT: Women often talk about being angry about being receptacles. In a sense, that's what they are—just a place for men to get rid of their excitement without having to do anything with the being of the person. I'm angry with women for being vulnerable enough to let it be carried out and, worse, to invite it.
THERAPIST: And that makes you feel bad about yourself that you were inviting it—the alternative of being unnoticed was such a painful choice.

THURSDAY

PATIENT: I'll spend five minutes complaining about the process and then get to work. It's like any work. I have to talk a bit at a time and I hate it. I think I should be able to be brilliant and wonderful and not have to work. I had dinner with Karl [classmate]. It was awkward at first. Then it was OK and a lot of stuff came up. I don't want to deal with it. I like it better when all this is under wraps. When I left Tuesday, your last statement made me feel bad. It's a deplorable situation when a woman lets herself be used as a receptacle. You said what I did as a kid. You men blame everything on women [a tone of pseudo-outrage]. I don't want to be teasing Jim (housemate) or have to think about it. I got over being angry with you. It's true to say I invited that response. No. It sounds defensive, but it's not true. What you said was the alternative was so painful—not teasing. It's hard to survive the isolation. I couldn't—physically even. It was too much. [Pause] It seemed so real. It was true to me at the time. It's no longer true. I don't have to be isolated, and if I did, I have the strength to deal with it. Then I didn't. It's a sad state of affairs, the way things were. [Sigh]

THERAPIST: Your sigh is your feeling about the "sad state of affairs"?

PATIENT: I was thinking what could have changed it. A lot of things. But they weren't there. My mother wasn't there to watch over me. She just wasn't there. . . . I was thinking on the way home what you said puts it in a different light. My anger toward my brother was mitigated. He had no supervision, no rules or guidance. We were all there together. [Sigh] I don't like the way he treated me. I really don't like him. I can see he was a kid too—a kid supported and maintained to have the idea he could do whatever he wanted. . . . After dinner with Karl—oh, it came up in a dream about Jim. I was nervous how Jim would be. I hadn't told him I was going out with Karl, although he knew Karl called. Jim came out of the room, and I worried he'd be jealous. That's how it was in the past with my family—jealousy.

THERAPIST: On whose part?

PATIENT: My brother's. When I was in high school and college everyone let me know my place was to be with my dad and my brother. Any boy I brought home was not good enough because he was a threat. Once when I was home on a visit, a man I was going with called me and asked me to come back because he was lonely. I wouldn't. He had a bad temper, and I was glad to get away. My brother heard me talk and said, "You know where your place is." In a dream I had last night, I was on the floor picking up something. Jim came over. I put my arm around his leg. Only it wasn't his leg, it was his crotch. When I realized it I tried to back off, but he wouldn't let me. I was trying to give him an affectionate gesture, let him know I had not gone, and then it got misplaced from Karl to Jim. But where does it come from? You're suggesting it's from my living with my family—my memories. In the dream one thing was apparent about making mistakes. My first was misconstruing where I placed my cheek. Then his in not letting it go. That is like my brother. I was not trying to get my face near his genitals. I was trying to share affection. That's what I was trying to do in the dream as well.

THERAPIST: In the dream, what were you doing to begin with? [Throughout the session Nancy has been carrying forward with little need for encouragement or focus. I wanted her to remain in touch with the dream imagery and I was curious about the beginning image, which had not been clear to me.]

PATIENT: I don't know. I was down on my knees picking up something. A note card maybe. He comes in. I want to make a gesture of affection, put my arm out and lean my face against—it would be his knee or upper calf. Then the size perspective changed, from child to adult. It's important because that's what gets played out here-feeling childish. [Pause] I just had a question: Do I understand the importance of what I'm saying? [Sigh] The answer is no. Like when I say something, and you say it back to me and then I see it.

THERAPIST: Are you asking me to say it?

PATIENT: Perhaps. [Hesitant]

THERAPIST: Do you want me to call attention to the longings that were so strong for you as a child? [Inviting without pushing]

PATIENT: My immediate response is to say no! Don't. That's stuff I don't want to touch [playful tone]. But if I don't, they'll keep coming up misplaced into an adult context, won't they?

THERAPIST: Yes.

PATIENT: Okay. So let's start with Number 1. You can go ahead and state it if you want. [Giggling] I can't.
THERAPIST: A longing to have somebody else take the lead and the responsibility?
[The interchange has taken on a playful quality. I was a participant in the playful enactment. I addressed the issue that seemed to me most immediately manifest in the intersubjective context.]

PATIENT: That's not so bad. Seems pretty normal for a kid, huh? So what's another? One thing that's clear is my wanting to be close to people, to be treated tenderly and affectionately. [Pause] [Sigh]
[I could easily pick up on the theme of wanting a positive attachment experience—the frustration of her mother's stiffening when Nancy reached for her leg, as in a model scene that had been worked with extensively. The desperate seeking of intimacy with the other available family members—all male—was a natural consequence. Nancy's long silence may have been an expectation of this familiar theme being reactivated.]

PATIENT: Are there worse ones that are scarier? These don't seem so scary.
[I assumed Nancy was saying she was ready to deal with a new problem area.]
THERAPIST: One longing might be to explore things that are unknown and scary.

PATIENT: Right. And not to have to do it alone!
THERAPIST: Yeah . . . and a man's crotch could be just such an area of curiosity and interest.

PATIENT: It seems reasonable that it would be. [Giggle] And breasts and bottoms—everything that's covered up I'd want to understand [sigh].
THERAPIST: Your sigh?

PATIENT: No way to do that that doesn't make me feel depraved. It makes sense. A child wants to see adult bodies and her own body. To do it and get rid of fears. My parents feared an interest in my body and others would lead to depravity. I don't know what it would be.

THERAPIST: What form could the depravity take?
[Nancy was using distancing speech forms—"A child wants" rather than "I wanted." I could have commented on this, but I chose not to, assuming she would use more direct speech as she became more comfortable with this "unknown and scary" area of exploration.]

PATIENT: Yeah. I don't know. [Pause] For Mother and me, being covered always. I never saw my mother's breasts until she was in her 50s. I could say I never saw my father naked but in tight revealing jockey shorts. And the time he got so mad because I walked in on him in the bathroom and stood staring aghast at his genitals. It makes me mad. There was nothing wrong with his not locking the door. It was me! And now I have this interest. It has become very important, everything now has a sexual genital flavor.

THERAPIST: And seems to retain the flavor of either "it's your fault" or "it's not your fault, it's the fault of someone who won't take responsibility."

PATIENT: That's what it had. What am I supposed to do with that? [argumentative] That's the way the messages came across to me.

THERAPIST: In your dream, you do parcel it out in a clear fashion.
[Nancy had been associating in a relatively free, open fashion. Then her anger mounted, and she became mildly provocative. I had the choice of either directing her attention to her argumentativeness with me as a recrudescence of her anger at her father (something I had done many times in the past) or trying to get more work done in associating to and exploring the meaning of her dream. As the hour was drawing to an end, and a weekend break was coming, I chose to remind her of the progress evident in her dream in which she assigns responsibility clearly. Prior to this she could only ruminate and fume

about her sense that all responsibility was placed on her and women as seducers of men.]

PATIENT: Yeah. What are you suggesting? I could have as a kid? Or I could parcel it out now and I'm not?
THERAPIST: How does it sit with you?

PATIENT: I don't think I could have as a kid.
THERAPIST: Um-hm. [Meaning agreement]

PATIENT: I think I could now. But I get caught in it. I did when I left Tuesday. I started thinking, "It takes two to tango." Then I lose it, and I'm back to "It's all my problem." Then I think, "Kids need adults to learn." It's a real problem for that not to be available.
THERAPIST: Yes.

PATIENT: I can take responsibility for wanting to know about everything.
[Nancy begins to sort out her thinking, how she goes back and forth with blame. She identifies parental responsibility in a general sense—"kids need adults." I affirm her recognition of this, and she shifts to the personal pronoun in saying, "I can take responsibility (for her curiosity)."]

PATIENT: I was a very curious little girl. But curious isn't perverted. If it becomes perverted, it's because something is wrong.
THERAPIST: Our time is up.

PATIENT: Let me say one more time I hate this work [good-naturedly]—the work I love to hate.
[Nancy returns to the resentment toward the analyst that remained unexplored when I chose to return to the dream.]

Through the clinical material, I have tried to illustrate that in exploratory psychotherapy, therapists can work with defensive activities as with any other experience. The problem of what patients don't want themselves or their therapists to know remains as critical a matter as when analytic theory began. But the view I offer here places defensive activities in the broader context of an aversive motivational system. Infants are born with the capacity to signal needs and desires and to signal their distress when needs are not met. Thus, aversiveness is an intersubjective experience of infant and caregiver from the beginning of life. Successful responsiveness to the infant's signals of need and aversiveness contributes to secure attachments and enhances self- and mutual regulation of affects. Failure to respond successfully contributes to insecure attachment and problems with self- and mutual regulation. The infant's aversive signals are affects and gestures—crying, anger, fear, sadness, shame—antagonism and withdrawal. To these the older toddler adds symbolic communication in the form of verbal expression, fantasies expressive of fears and anger, and complex play sequences alone or with peers. Gradually the very fabric of antagonism and avoidance becomes embedded in cognition and speech. This is the form therapists become involved in as patients like Nancy bring their forgetting, reluctance, obfuscating, denial and disavowal, their avoidance and preoccupations, into focus in their verbal, imagistic and gestural interchanges. These conventional modes of communication occur when patients are experiencing higher levels of consciousness, including the possibility of self-reflection. But all too often with all patients coping with heightened episodes of aversiveness and intense affective states, lower levels of consciousness predominate. More important than the occasional dip into lower levels of consciousness of the more integrated patients are the persistent or recurrent problems of borderline and dissociative patients. For these patients, the barrier against understanding, relatedness, and progress arises from disturbed self- and mutual regulation of affect and processing of information rather than "defense." For patients like Sister Mary, for whom lower levels of consciousness predominate with here and now, all or nothing, thinking, affect states, and absence of reflection, the problem shifts from what she doesn't want to let herself, me, or us know to the grave difficulty of letting the significance of anything be known. Containment, remaining with and living through the period in which lower levels of consciousness predominate must allow for self-righting to higher levels before exploring the patient's defense and resistance can be effective.

Repetitive focus on a patient's aversive experience can be itself a source of aversiveness. Jill, a successful professional, began her session, as was common for her, with a complaint about Cecile, her therapist. Cecile had been two minutes late and, in response to being asked about her feelings, Jill said, "If you cared about me you would be on time." Jill, who had for years been a serious alcoholic, had been helped to be sober and was a member of AA. She usually presented herself dressed like a homeless waif unless she had a professional appointment. Then she wore appropriate clothing selected by a shopper she hired but with rips in her hose. Cecile and Jill began to reexamine how Cecile's lateness triggered once again Jill's often reviewed neglect by her unfeeling, overworked, frazzled mother. Jill stopped and said, "This sounds like a drunkalogue. On and on about my mother." Cecile heard in Jill's reflective comment a call for a fresh approach. She said, "Do you mean that as we keep reviewing how I might be hurting or neglecting you like your mother, something is getting lost? That I am fond of you and you are fond of me never gets acknowledged and talked about." After a thoughtful pause, Jill said, "I feel like a tension has suddenly been relieved." Cecile responded, "Maybe you feel relieved that each time we talk about us it doesn't have to remind you of hurts and anger, but of the affection you can and do feel?" Jill, somewhat eager but also unsure, asked, "How do we talk about affection? This is new territory for me. I feel like I am standing in front of a vast field, and I don't know which way to go. I remember when I came home from school my mother would put my drawings on the refrigerator. I thought that meant she cared but when she didn't for the younger children, I thought she was only doing her duty. That's what I think of you when you are late. I'll need a lot of help to think any other way." Cecile ended the session saying, "Now that the tension is gone, you and I can be open to recognizing affection as well as hurts."

In this chapter, I have focused on therapists' recognition, tracking, and interpreting of aversive experience.

In chapter 9, I discuss more broadly the entire repertoire of therapists' spoken interventions.

CHAPTER 9

THE THERAPIST SPEAKS

TO THE QUESTION OF THE DIFFERENCE BETWEEN a psychotherapist and a psychoanalyst, a cynical answer has been "the therapist speaks." This critique had validity at a time when analysts might wait to speak only when they were able to provide an "exact interpretation" in a field uncontaminated by unnecessary gratification or knowledge of the analyst. My fellow analytic candidates in the 1950s would compete about whose training analyst could remain silent longest. Happily, this misguided attempt at neutrality and abstinence has long been superseded by a broad acknowledgment that ordinary human responsiveness facilitates rather than detracts from the progress of all exploratory therapies. So the therapist speaks and the analyst speaks! This chapter is about principles that guide therapists' communications.

I describe three perspectives from which therapists communicate to further therapeutic exploration. I choose to refer to communications rather than interpretations. A therapist's communications include all three meanings of interpretation and more besides. Therapists will explain the meaning of an association, a memory, an interaction, and an intervention. Interpreting meaning in this usage is to relate an experience occurring in one context to one or more other contexts, thereby broadening understanding. Therapists also will relate communications expressed in one "language" or mode (such as dream imagery, gestural action, humor, metaphor and symbolization as well as linear syntactic verbalization) to another mode or modes. This is the meaning of interpreter as translator. Therapists' interventions additionally may involve interpretation in the sense of the creative art of a conductor conveying his vision of a Beethoven symphony or a ballerina expressing her vision of a wounded swan. In these visions, conductor and ballerina remain true to the score or choreography but add something that vitalizes the uniqueness of the performance. In comparable fashion, therapists remain true to the "text" of their patients' experiences and their experiences together but add a personal way of constructing conceptually and verbally that vitalizes the uniqueness of their joint endeavor. This last form of creative interpretation facilitates the emergence of two subjectivities through an exploration directed to elucidate one.

Interpretations provide many of the explicit forms of a therapist's communications. Nonetheless effective interpersonal communication requires a foundation of implicit forms of exchanges. If the most careful process notes of a session are compared with a tape recording, striking differences appear. The process notes, whether written during the session or from memory afterward, will reveal the therapist's speaking an average of 5 to 12 times. The tape will reveal the many ums, uh-huhs, and ohs that considerably increase the number of therapist speech elements. The process notes will portray the interchange as patient speaks, followed by therapist speaks, followed by patient, and so on. A tape recording will convey the pauses between speakers that are long and awkward, a "pulling teeth" type of exchange; or short pauses and staccato statements, a heated exchange often with interruptions of one another; or a slow, deliberate, thoughtful type of easy comfortable rhythm. More important, if the flow of mutual exchanges changes, a tape recording helps to identify the moment in the session when the change occurred. If the session is videotaped and therapist and patient are viewed on a split screen, the facial expressions add a further dimension to the affective concordance or discordance taking place. Additionally a completely out-of-awareness gestural communication becomes evident as shared body tensions or relaxed parallel hand-to-face scratches add to the mutuality of the exchanges, or animation of face and gesture of one and that expressionless face and gesture of the other provides evidence that although the two are talking to one another, their affective connection is poor.

Returning to verbal communication, therapists following the techniques espoused here address patients from three perspectives. The most frequent perspective derives from the significance placed on the empathic mode of perception. Once therapists learn to listen primarily to discern a patient's point of view, they will naturally formulate responses that convey that mode of attending. Phrases such as, "So what you're telling me is . . ." or "Oh, the way you experienced it was . . ." or "In your view, there was a lot of confusion between . . ." or "At the moment, you felt you simply couldn't do otherwise than . . ." serve as introductions to validate therapists' understanding and open the subject for further inquiry.

The final exchanges with Nancy in the session reported in chapter 8 provide an example of interventions from an empathic vantage point. Demonstrating a great deal of courage and trust, Nancy had opened to us a frank look at her brother's sexual exploitation of her. Contrasting the experience with her brother with her age-appropriate sexual exploration at ten or eleven with her friend Margaret, Nancy stated, "It was not dirty. It was clean. There were no secretions. With my brother, it was his ejaculation that was sick, gross. As you said before [an appreciation of her feeling of my being with her], in the play with Margaret, we were equals. My brother would rub against me. Against my leg, my stomach, until he had ejaculations. I felt very dirty and used."

Sensing as best I could from within her perspective, I concluded that in Nancy's rendering of the abuse, unlike previous references, she was not in danger of becoming overwhelmed if I followed up her opening. Accordingly, I said, "You didn't have a sense of being appreciated for yourself but for the purpose you served?" She responded, "Women often talk about being angry about being receptacles. In a sense, that's what they are—just a place for men to get rid of their excitement without having to deal with the being of the person. I'm angry at men for taking women as receptacles. I'm angry at women for being vulnerable enough to let it be carried out and, worse, to invite it."

I hear in what Nancy is saying her deeply felt hurt, shame, and anger and her generalizing from herself to "women." Still, from her perspective I want to bring her back to her own experience as she is presenting it now and also draw on our prior understanding of her motivation to be involved with her brother as a source of needed attachment. I state, "And that makes you feel bad about yourself, that you were inviting it—the alternative of being unnoticed was such a painful choice."

These interventions by me are made at a point in Nancy's therapy when we had shared a great deal of information about Nancy's past, the inferences she had formed, and our mutual sense of being able to explore collaboratively. The complexity of these interpretations contrasts with the simplicity of more echolike encouragements therapists make at other times. Comments such as "That sounds like you were very disappointed, could you say more?" or "How did you feel about the interruption to your trip?" or, even more simply, "Really angry?" This technique of responding very close to a patient's statement was found by its originator Carl Rogers to encourage in the patient a sense of being closely attended and understood. Critics have charged this approach with being too nice, rather simple-mindedly accepting anything a patient says, and potentially being patronizing. When a patient's affect is being correctly identified and restated in a matter-of-fact tone of acknowledgment, I believe that the restatement conveys both "I hear you" and "Your emotion is of singular importance." Nothing saccharin or condescending in that! Nonetheless, a restricted ritualistic dose of "So what you are saying is . . ." would not be sympathizing and pacifying as critics claim, it would be boring and aggravating. Maintaining a perspective from within a patient's perspective does not constrain a therapist to contorted circumlocutions. The fluidity of responses I made to Nancy and other examples throughout the book attest to my belief that therapists should remain free of ritualistic constraint. Critics do have a point, however. Relatively simple restatements offer little or no challenge to the patient's momentary point of view. In fact, that *is* their value—promoting safety through a sense of acceptance to further explore the momentary perspective. More complex interpretations like my connecting Nancy's shame at "inviting" her brother's abuse and her desperate need for attachment does challenge her to identify two disparate motives and contexts operative in the same enactment. The two other perspectives for a therapist's communication that I describe now are more directly challenging.

Second in frequency to therapists' communicating from the patient's perspective are therapists using their own subjective experience to illuminate a recognizable pattern, or to communicate personal feelings, appraisals, or impressions. Therapists turn to their own perspective many times but may or may not choose to speak from it rather than returning to the patient's perspective to speak. A therapist may say to herself, "I'm surprised that my patient took offense at my commenting on her having been a good student." Knowing that her face had registered her surprise at the patient's burst of anger, she chose to say, "I'm puzzled that you are upset at my comment about your being a good student. Could you help me understand what troubles you about it?" Sometimes, the impressions therapists form as they step away from the patient's experience open the way to a connection hitherto unappreciated. The therapist may then somewhat excitedly say, "Oh, I see the same pattern of hurting you and then seducing you back was followed by your brother as well as your father. Boy you really got a double dose of it." Another way that therapists turn to their own perspective is when their emotions are triggered either directly or inadvertently. A therapist's mild annoyance helped him to recognize that a patient's avoidant stance about acknowledging her fearfulness was related to her adherence to a false idealization of him. He suggested, "I think you break off telling me how frightened you become because you see me as someone who has managed to go through life without ever experiencing fear. I believe you think I wouldn't be able to appreciate your anxiety, and you will only feel humiliated at revealing yourself to me."

At times, a therapist will experience an emotion that, although fully responsive to the context, has more to do with his own inclinations of the moment than the patient's direct or indirect triggering. For example, in a session with Nancy that had been going well, I became impatient at the slow pace of Nancy's working with a dream. Her reluctance to open herself to consider a possible sexual symbolism in any dream was well established. I was usually comfortable with her pacing. When in this session I became annoyed and pushy, I reacted more on the basis of my state of mind than whatever minimal cueing was arising from her. My reaction was like that moment when, driving behind a slow driver, caution says wait, and my foot hits the accelerator. Nancy's immediate response, "Again I feel trapped," confirmed the danger for her of being pressed to conform to the motives of another, of a man dealing with sex, a danger I knew well, but one that at that moment I was moved by my inner state to ignore.

A therapist's emotions and point of view can be evoked directly by a patient's direct assault on his worth or motives, and by threats of quitting, lawsuits, or suicide. A young woman was referred to me for intensive therapy by a colleague in another city who had been a close personal friend for many years. She had had to interrupt her four sessions a week treatment with him to marry a suitable young man whose profession brought him to Washington. For nine months, she poured out an endless series of complaints about Washington, my office, and me. I did my best to tolerate her provocations and to gain entry into their source. She threw back in my face most of the efforts I made to speak from her point of view. On one occasion, I said, "We certainly have a difficult time seeing eye to eye on anything." "We," she roared back, "there's no we here." My feelings shifted from puzzled and irritable to doubt and futility. I responded to her threats of quitting with fantasies of the relief that would provide me. As this reached a crisis point, she entered and, standing near my chair, said in a determined voice, "I demand that you tell me if treatment will help me. I will not continue unless you answer me!" After a brief moment of reflection, I answered, "I am convinced you can benefit from treatment. I am not convinced it should be with me." She said, "Thank you. I'll be back tomorrow."

The next day, she said she had thought about what I said and wanted to know why I thought maybe not with me. I told her I have been unable to understand what was transpiring between us and without that understanding, I doubted that progress could be made. She reopened the issue of missing her prior therapist but in a way that opened my eyes to my massive denial of the sadomasochistic nature of their relationship. They had fought about everything. He had accused her of symbolically trying to castrate him when he discovered his umbrella was missing. She had seen his active involvement through what I regard as wild and provocative "interpretations" as evidence of caring. Because I had been handpicked by him, she expected a continuation of a form of interaction she had come to value. This led to a frank and direct discussion on my part of my differing approach to treatment. To my amazement, the entire ambiance changed, and we began a very successful period of mutual exploration of problems in her marriage and the many holdovers of characterology issues from her childhood.

The threat of suicide constitutes a special pull on therapists' use of their own perspective. Appraising the seriousness of the danger is often difficult. The anxiety stirred in the therapist has considerable but far from reliable value as a guide. Having a patient commit suicide constitutes an assault on a therapist's belief in himself as well as a painful loss. Consequently, suicide as an act of vengeance for a therapist's failures has often been emphasized. Vengeance is a frequent component of suicide fantasies, as is the "beautiful corpse" that will inspire those who have been hurtful or neglectful to appreciate whom they have lost. The best way to regard suicidal ideation as a serious potential is, I believe, not that of vengeance or the evocation of guilt or remorse, but the powerful benefit envisioned to arise from escape from unbearable emotional (and/or physical) pain. I encourage therapists I supervise actively to envision their patients' and their own perspective. Entering the patient's state of mind, they must fully appreciate the powerful lure of the vision of escape, tranquility, and finality, whatever embellishments of vengeance, afterlife, or reunion with lost love ones are added.

Therapists treating suicidal patients must sense the struggle over "Can I bear it any longer," the "it" referring to a deep, seemingly irreparable assault on the patient's sense of self. Only in this way can therapists convey to a patient their connectedness at a moment of desperation, a connectedness that *might* forestall an irreversible act. Or the connectedness *might not,* and therapists must be prepared for that possibility, even, at times, that likelihood. I advise therapists to picture the situation in which their patient is no longer alive, to open their feelings to imagine their mourning, their hurt, their anger. I believe that this foreshadowed mind drama helps therapists to reflect on their limitations and to know that despite the battering to their confidence that losing a patient through suicide will cause, they can, will, and must survive. This preparation has two advantages. First, therapists are enabled to struggle directly with the problem the patient's precarious hold on life presents without denial—a preparation that will help therapists to maintain their professional equilibrium. Second, a therapist who can face the patient's distress and desire for escape without denial can much more effectively evaluate the degree of risk present and the appropriate steps needed: medication, high frequency of contact, notification of family members, hospitalization for the patient and consultation for the therapist.

Therapists benefit with all patients, but particularly with more troubled patients, from learning to be adept at following themes in a session from the patient's point of view and also keeping a grasp on their own perspective. Yet the art of adjusting to the need to communicate in ways that move treatment forward lies in therapists' nimble ability to shift perspectives intuitively. During a clinical experience with a high-functioning professional woman, I found it necessary to shift from the immediacy of my perspective to hers. Before my planned absence of a week, I had followed my usual procedure of giving her a written times-I-will-be-away notice months ahead, talked about my upcoming absence during preceding sessions, and at the door stated the date when I would see her again. On my return, she entered looking distressed and fuming angrily. She described having come to my office, finding the door locked, and banging impotently on the door. She felt badly hurt and betrayed. I sputtered something about being sorry and how awful it was for her to expect to find me and be confronted by a locked door. She wasn't sure she could ever forgive me. She was not comforted at all by what I said. How could I do that to her? I explained that I had not meant to do it, that I had taken the precaution of the times-away notice and the mentioning during the hour and at the door. She looked at me as if I had been talking Greek, and I finally understood the need to shift from my point of view, which had been defensive and self-righteous, to hers. I said, "Regardless of what I meant and what I did, what matters is I failed to communicate to you that I would be gone. I knew and know you needed to know that, and I didn't succeed in having you know." With that clarity on my part and acknowledgment to her, we were able to restore our base for resuming a collaborative exploration.

Mr. R, another high-functioning professional, presented an even greater requirement for me to shift perspectives. He entered treatment because of irritability and depression that he said he knew about only because his wife had told him. His mother had been frequently depressed, his father controlling, obsessional, and phobic. This picture of his family came to him from his older sister; he had no memory of his parents' problems. His motto was, "Don't get mad, get even." In the treatment, he sulked, pouted, and missed hours—one for one I missed. He yawned when discussing anything emotional and fell silent, often for extended periods. During the silences, he reviewed his day's schedule. On reconnecting with me he had no memory of the preceding discussion.

He began many sessions stating that he had not thought of what we had talked about, or that he had a dream but did not remember it. What was striking to me about this experienced scientist was that whether the subject was the previous hour or *an unremembered dream*, he expected *me* to know what it was and to tell him. Much of his impact on me tended to pull me into an irritable depression with him. My working alternative was to do what I could to supply the missing memory links and build a continuity that he could use and we could use. I would tell him what I remembered we were talking about before the yawn and silence or what we discussed in the previous hour. But an unremembered, unreported dream? What was that about? This puzzling expectation of an adult signaled to me a request that I fulfill the expectation of a small child that his mother (caregiver) carry him in her mind in the most profound sense of being known. Mr. R was telling me that he hoped I would respond to him as would a fully attached mother who really knows her baby and his particularities—a knowing that a seriously depressed mother cannot achieve. Nor can a therapist truly provide it. What I could do was not get caught up in a battle about it and oversimplify the enactment occurring between us as resistance or "merely" defensiveness. I could hold him and us in my mind to the extent I could and ungrudgingly offer him my perspective of what I could remember that had transpired between us. Then when his grudging get-even sulk was available to us, I could shift to seeing it from his perspective. I could then follow up with the negative impact on me, and us, especially how he squeezed all joy out of our work and how his life is lived as if in a mausoleum.

THERAPIST: [Picking up from the previous session when he allowed himself to recognize his previously denied capacity to initiate, I said] At the end of yesterday's session, you said you know how to initiate. You did it with your course. I agreed, and you countered. But it wasn't fun.
PATIENT: Fun is not sanctioned.

THERAPIST: You know it is by me. You comment obliquely about my swimming pool, and my interest in sailing and art. [Here I am speaking from my perspective to move the narrative forward.]
PATIENT: I assiduously avoid using you. I don't allow myself. Your way is not sanctioned. You couldn't be a good parent.

THERAPIST: You feel you gave me an opening, and I didn't follow an exact channel. [Now I shift to his perspective as I understand it.]
PATIENT: I can't accept anything that deviates from the script. Get it, and I go on. If I don't, the whole thing falls apart. I can't adapt to a different response. [Yawn]

THERAPIST: Or it's hard for you to. It makes you anxious. [I regard his yawn as an indication of mounting anxiety triggering a desire to withdraw into pessimism.]
PATIENT: Yeah. My father's inflexibility. Avoiding anything that's

> new. The model for the script here is that it's open-ended. Each statement opens the potential for going off in all directions. That makes me anxious. Like you going off in all directions. I want you right here! Not going off sailing or playing tennis. [My shifting perspectives help me to stay with him. He quickly emerges from a felt need to withdraw and forcefully expresses a strongly felt desire: "I want you right here!"]

All patients benefit from therapists speaking from their point of view. With more disturbed, traumatized patients, empathic understanding is often difficult to achieve and more needed. Likewise, all patients benefit from therapists speaking from their point of view frankly and honestly without pretence or lecturing and with minimal dissimulation. With more disturbed patients, therapists often find honesty and frankness to be more difficult but often more crucial to the sense of safety required for exploration. Therapists behave foolishly and ineffectually if they fail to acknowledge and bring into the foreground what they are obviously communicating by facial expression, body language, and vocal tone. Inevitably in any exploratory treatment, therapists are likely to reveal that they feel worried, wounded, angry, sad, confused, physically unwell, or that they are pleased, fond, amused, interested, excited. I am reminded of a story about Freud saying to a patient who had finally fully appreciated an interpretation "This calls for a celebration; I'm going to get myself a cigar."

The most difficult stress for me in treating Sonya (chapter 5) was the up-and-down pattern of the early phase of her therapy. After an initial phase of almost total silence on Sonya's part, we began to have sessions in which we could share moments of interactive dialogue. But I found that these "good" sessions were invariably followed by sessions of intense gloom. I began to anticipate these despair-filled sessions with a sinking sensation in the pit of my stomach. Sonya would press me to join her in her total hopelessness and pessimism. In this instance, taking a perspective guided by hers and speaking from it was easily done—I had been drawn deeply into the experience. The problem for me was how to find an alternative perspective of hope and efficacy from which to speak. I knew that

Sonya's messages to me were both "Will you take me at my word that I am miserably unhappy and allow *me*, not my mother and brother, to receive care and help rather than having to provide it to others?" and "No one helps me, everyone expects too much, and no one wants to or *can* affect in the least the depressive gloom and doom I am resigned to."

Especially when confronted with her subtle hints at abandoning the treatment and less than subtle references to suicide, I was confronted with the painful possibility that my faith that I could ultimately help her might be unsustainable. In my inner monologue, I could draw on my own early experiences when I had learned to sustain my equilibrium, even my sanity, while listening to the complaints of troubled people. I had inferred that I could have a positive effect on my troubled family members. Drawing on these childhood experiences helped but was not enough. Sonya thoroughly distrusted having me assume a role of either benevolent caregiver or analytic explorer. Consequently, my empathic effort to be true to her affect state afforded no sense of efficacy or competence. She felt trapped, and I felt trapped. To escape, I was forced back to search within myself to establish a perspective from which I could speak. For an expression of optimism about eventual help for her, I reminded myself of my many successful experiences as a therapist and of Sonya's many abilities and what was, to me, her essential likeableness. I could then say that although we shared moments of feeling helpless to relieve her despair, I did not share her hopelessness. Using my own experience, I could say I knew that attempts to struggle against feeling helpless and sinking into pessimism could succeed. To myself I had to acknowledge that my verbal statement of reassurance to Sonya was probably as much a statement to myself as to her.

Some responses of therapists are difficult to acknowledge to themselves and to their patients. The arousal of strong affect of any sort, whether hypomanic or sexual excitement, romantic attachment, revulsion, rage, fear, contempt, or despair or the absence of interest or caring, all place therapists in a difficult position to be either open to their patient's subjectivity or to manage their own response. My experience is that the sooner therapists can identify their developing affective state, the sooner they can identify the context in which the feeling is being evoked. The task then is to describe the interplay or enactment from the therapist's perspective and, if possible, to identify what has triggered the therapist's response while keeping some focus on the patient's perspective.

A woman therapist was treating Terence, a successful businessman who at times would suddenly begin to describe lurid tales of his sadistic fantasies and actions with children. She felt extreme revulsion but was able, with the help of supervision, to recognize that these flights into sadism followed experiences in which he had felt humiliated by a dominating authority. This recognition gave her enough conceptual distance to use her revulsion as a signal to identify and interpret the pattern before she was overwhelmed with loathing and disgust, and he with the need to overdramatize his evil intent. Terence was able to express fondness and appreciation of the therapist but also could attack and threaten her to the point where she would feel shaken during and after the session. He would be insulting, calling her a computer chip, or he would threaten to grab her. She struggled with a sense of impotent paralysis in the face of these provocations. With the help of supervision, she insisted that he give her a chance to identify what had happened to set him off. Had he experienced her as failing him in some way, as hurting him or depriving him? Was he attempting to restore his pride by humiliating and tormenting her—at the risk of spoiling and destroying her effectiveness, her good will, and even her being? In this example, as with most situations of overwhelming domination–submission enactments, the problem is how to restore the balance of a collaborative give and take without reshuffling the deck back and forth between who is dominant and who submissive. The flexibility to move between an empathic focus on the patient's experience, an introspective focus on the therapist's experience, and an awareness of the interplay between them helps to unlock the binding power of tormentor–tormented, victimizer–victim enactments.

I have described therapists speaking from a perspective drawn from their appraisal of their patients' point of view (an empathic mode of perception), from their own perspective, or sometimes both. Therapists participating in the dialogue may express themselves after thoughtful deliberation or more extemporaneously. The form of communication from either perspective may use more formal syntax or more personalized vernacular. My own experience and incidents related to me by other therapists—sometimes with pride, sometimes with embarrassment—affirm that not infrequently therapists find themselves saying something that seemed to just "come out of their mouths." These utterances usually evoke surprise, even startle to either or both therapist and patient. We (Lichtenberg, Lachmann, and Fosshage) have titled these therapist communications "disciplined spontaneous engagements." "Disciplined" indicates the utterances remain within the boundaries of professional ethics and practices and within the tolerance of the particular patient at the particular time. "Spontaneous" refers to therapists' comments, facial expressions, and actions having the eruptive character of an unsuppressed emotional upsurge. Comparable to a flash of wit in a repartee, these outside-the-book communicative moments are embedded in the interactive or dramatic aspect of therapy rather than the contemplative and investigative.

At a point in Veronica's treatment (chapter 2), she began to be insulting and provocative. The main thrust of her disdainful remarks referred to me as weak and ineffectual, having no flair, and being in a conventional marriage with a compliant "nice" little wife. Efforts on my part either to understand the current trigger for her assault or to link it to past events led to further sarcastic rejection, an enactment of my ineffectualness. I had tended to attribute her upset to her well-established, desperate need to feel me with her. In one session, as her abuse poured out, I sensed her experiencing a sadistic contentment with her abrasive attack. I erupted in a loud, angry voice, "OK, if what you want to do is fight, I'll fight with you." After a moment of startle, her response was equally dramatic and surprising: "Oh, good. Now I don't have to worry about hurting you!"

As we both settled down, we began an exploration that led to her belief that I was a weak doormat like her mother. She hated her mother's weakness. In her rage at her mother's needy pursuit of her, she would be nasty to her mother in a manner similar to her father's unbridled eruptions. She then felt guilty and worried about how mean and out of control she got with her mother and no one else. Looking back at the content of my eruptive comment, I was interpreting the view I had come to of her motivation—that she wanted to fight. When I missed the cue and didn't either identify the motive (an exploratory failure) or engage in a fight (enter into the enactment), she upped the force of the message to a sadistic provocation and began to enjoy it. That her motive had become to insist on a hostile interchange was apparent from her provocativeness. What was less apparent to me was that she wanted me to demonstrate that I, too, could and would fight. I was not committed characterologically to submit to mistreatment and only whine about it.

An example of a disciplined, spontaneous engagement occurred in my treatment of an adolescent girl. Lisa entered treatment with the support of her mother and the reluctance of her father. Attractive, bright, and creative, she complained about a quiet, dull depression and a feeling of being isolated from peers. For several years she had been unable to manage bulimic bingeing and purging. She felt she was unlike most teenagers in that she really loved her parents. She felt sorry for her mother who saw herself as the least successful member of a brilliant family. She respected her father's intelligence and struggle to rise above humble beginnings. They cared about her and were kind to her, and her complaints seemed petty to her.

Lisa and I quite obviously liked each other and formed a bond that allowed her to tell me many intimate details about her life and feelings. Nonetheless, her dull depression and bulimia remained unaffected. More and more we could recognize intellectually how bothered she was by her mother's low self-esteem. In a session taken up mostly with tracking the most recent episode of bulimia, we found ourselves having a long silence of discouragement as the end approached. Suddenly, in a voice of direct appeal she had never used, she asked, "What shall I do?" Spontaneously I answered, "Feel!" "Oh," she responded, "I should feel" and left. The next session she reported that at the time of the day when she would purge, she had confronted her mother about her disappointment in her. To her surprise she had spoken angrily. Now she felt sad, really sad, as if a whole way of being had been broken through. The session ended with her crying poignantly. Based, I assumed, on her European upbringing, Lisa routinely shook hands with me on leaving. This time the handshake rather than ritual was accompanied by her looking directly at me with appealing, tear-filled eyes. I held her hand in my right hand and automatically found my left hand enclosing her hand in a gentle caress until it seemed we both knew it was time to end.

In another experience with Lisa, I chose to contain my emotions and to refrain from verbally addressing the enactment taking place. A year after beginning therapy, Lisa, wearing short shorts, began waving her legs about and thrusting her chest forward—all sexually provocative. With an adult patient whose comparable behavior would probably be less obvious, I would describe and discuss what was being created between us. With Lisa, however, I regarded her body messages as a revelation largely to herself of a developmental thrust rather than a communication to me of an erotic transference. As Lisa's body was speaking its sensual message, her conversation was unchanged in tone or content. I stayed with the tone and content knowing that I might be mistaken and that an erotic message to me could be consciously or unconsciously intended. My assessment that a developmental pathway was opening was confirmed when, two weeks later, Lisa told me that she discovered that boys who had previously ignored her were looking at her, and that one boy asked her to go to a movie. Her message was going to where it needed to go developmentally—to peers.

With Bruce, an older teenager, a disciplined, spontaneous engagement came early in the treatment and set the tone for the years of successful exploration to come. Bruce had had a drug-induced psychotic episode in his first year of college. He had wanted to go to another therapist—one known to be more directive and interactional—but his hospital therapist and his parents had insisted he come to me. He came to his early sessions in ragged cutoff jeans, with hair unkempt and a rebellious contemptuous demeanor. As his provocations mounted, in a tone of some exasperation, I told him that I knew he felt stuck with me, and he certainly was helping to create a situation in which I would feel I was stuck with him. Although it would make it easier, he didn't have to like me for us to do what we had to do to help him. What he did have to do was to keep working at letting me in on what was going on with him, and I would do my part in letting him know whatever I thought would be helpful. This spontaneous outpouring of mine—a mix of an authoritative and authoritarian stance—established a pact between us that held as a working model between us while Bruce completed college, graduate school, and worked out his brutal domination of anyone he saw as weak and vulnerable. Two months before we were to end, with Bruce moving far away to take a good professional position, I spontaneously responded to one of his familiar put-downs: "Look, you have a choice. You can leave, maintaining your stance that you were and are stuck with me and don't like me, or you can try out what it might be like for you, for us, to feel friendly and part friends. Either way, you will take away with you the great gains you have made." Bruce's immediate reaction was, "Nah," but the next day he decided he would try out seeing whether he could let up on his hostility and see what would happen. He added that after all, he might want to keep in touch and have me know how he fared in his new life, which he did.

Mr. Titus was a creative entrepreneur. He struggled with a broad spectrum of self-esteem problems. Although a sincere and dedicated patient, making changes was difficult for him. Nonetheless, over time he made considerable progress in understanding the nature of current problems and their link to his mother's bipolar illness and father's literal and figurative deaf ear to his son's ability and needs. The affective regulation that seemed most intransigent was Mr. Titus's eruptive rage toward his son for blocking him in being able to do something Mr. Titus wanted to do. We knew of an earlier manifestation of his eruptive rage in frequent episodes in childhood when he was forced into periods of physical constraint by his mother's collapses into depressive exhaustion.

Mr. Titus's wife frequently came between him and his son to protect the child, but enough episodes of sadistic abuse occurred to worry both Mr. Titus and me. He was describing an episode of his son's being balky and challenging. Mr. Titus's anger erupted, and he pinned the boy's shoulders against the car. I listened with a feeling of impotent rage at the sadism involved. As the session was coming to an end, I found myself having a fantasy, seemingly disconnected, of the weekend when I would be engaged in the friendly rivalry I had with my son at tennis. Sitting up on the couch, Mr. Titus turned to me and, in a way he had never done before asked, "What should I do about my son? I don't want to hurt him." "Be his friend!" flowed out of my mouth without reflection or my knowledge of its source in my "disconnected" fantasy. Mr. Titus took hold of the concept of friendship like a drowning man grabbing a life preserver. He began to recognize how much friendship, friendliness, and shared goodwill were lacking across many motivational areas in his life.

What explains therapists' sudden shifts from more deliberate, thoughtful, nuanced communications to more spontaneous eruptive interventions? What led me in many examples I have provided to operate more improvisationally than is my usual practice? Clearly, therapists are not trained to tell a patient who is likely to cut herself, "Do it now," a pessimistic depressed young woman trapped in her own pathos, "You look like a sad little kitten," or a nun belligerently denying a mutual seduction with a young woman, "You may want to insist it is only an exchange of affection, but when you are naked in bed together and masturbating I call it sexual!" Although such dramatic utterances are not a part of the prescribed technique of psychotherapy, they are a common component of folklore—at least during my years of training, they were the substance of many lively stories. However dramatic or witty they may be in the telling, they represent, I believe, serious efforts on the part of therapists to escape a sinking sense of potentially impending disaster and futility. Disciplined spontaneous engagements reflect therapists drawing on their humanity at a moment when they despair of operating within the boundaries of a usual patient approach. They are something like the warning scream of a passenger in a car who recognizes that neither she nor the driver were reacting to an imminent danger ahead. An oft-repeated story is of Heinz Kohut telling a patient who bragged about making his session on time by speeding all across Chicago that he was going to give him a most important interpretation, namely: "You are an idiot!" From my exploration of the examples of my own "eruptions" and those of others, I conclude that they occur when an enactment is taking place that involves a sense of conscious or unconscious evasiveness on the part of both partners in the dyad. Then therapists experience internally the sense that they can no longer go along with the illusion of benignity without doing something more or different. "Hanging in" with a standard technique gives way to an immediate quest for authenticity. The quest may turn out to be helpful as in the examples I have given, or quixotic or harmful, but at the moment the therapist waives the risk and proceeds. The safeguard for "Feel," "Be his friend," or "OK, if what you want to do is fight, I'll fight with you!" or "You are an idiot!" is the consistent inquiry and sensitivity to the point of view of the patient and the relational realm that has grown out of the therapeutic collaboration. The spontaneous eruption may seem to be out of the blue, but it never is. Whether from an empathic vantagepoint or the vantagepoint of their own views and reactions or via spontaneous engagements, therapists speak from a context of caring, relatedness, and a spirit of inquiry. In the preceding chapters, I have presented guides to how therapists listen, what aspects of the complex communications warrant their focus, and how they respond to a patient's message, their own introspection, and the interplay that has emerged during their experience together. In the final chapter and coda, I will describe guidelines for evaluating progress. Evaluating progress is not a separate activity to be done at a particular interval or at the end of treatment. Rather, evaluating progress is an integral aspect of every session in that the most immediate way a therapist and a patient can know the impact each is having on the other is by tracking what follows.

CHAPTER 10

EVALUATING PROGRESS

WE CAN REGARD PROGRESS AS A MICROPROCESS, the result of one or more communications within a session, or more broadly, the cumulative effect over many sessions. My answer to a frequently asked question, "How does a therapist know if an intervention is beneficial?" is "See what comes next." Stated more formally, the tenth principle of technique is "We follow the sequence of our interventions and the patient's responses to them to evaluate their effect." In this chapter, I describe various ways to "see what comes next."

As fall began, Sonya (see chapter 5), after a period of improvement in mood assisted by antidepressive medication, began to sink deeply into depression. She knew about the therapeutic use of "lights" for seasonal depression but reiterated her pessimism that nothing would help. After a long silence, I asked about her medication. She was taking it but it was not helping. I suggested she call the neuropharmacologist for a reevaluation. Again, she refused, and we sat in a long, stalemated silence. As I looked questioningly over to her, our eyes met. I reacted facially to her painful expression. She asked, "What?" referring to my look. I spontaneously answered sympathetically, "You look like a sad little kitten!"—a metaphor I had never used before. After a more reflective silence, she stated, "I'll go but I don't want to." Relieved but sensing something else in her reluctance, I noted that I knew her pessimism was related to her mother having a medicine cabinet full of meds that Sonya felt did her mother no good. I also knew she hated taking medicine and hated to think of herself as sick. I asked, "Is there something else?" She responded with unusual directness; "I don't like Dr. N. I don't want to go back to him." With equal directness, I responded, "You don't have to go back to him. I can refer you to someone else." "OK," she answered. She accepted the name of a woman neuropharmacologist to whom she went to consult. The new antidepressant triggered a dramatic upsurge in her mood, activating her interest in dating for the first time in years. A further unexpected response was her acquiring a kitten. The ups and downs of the "kitty's" health and playful doings provided a conversational subject that reduced silences. Bringing into the foreground stories of the kitten served as a model scene we continued to cocreate and could be used as a proxy for talking about development and parenting—a positive counterpart of her negative view of her unremembered younger years.

Obvious progress is being documented in this brief segment of Sonya's therapy. My main purpose in presenting it is to examine the microprocesses that characterize the interplay in the dialogic exchange. The session begins with a familiar enactment. Sonya indicates a problem—the seasonally determined sinking mood. We then play out my offer to provide help and her characteristic refusal. Her rejection sinks us both into a stalemate of futility. Our established rhythm dictates that I wait for a sign from her of a desire to resume contact. The sign comes in the form of our eyes meeting and our shared facial expression of sadness. Her "What?" indicates to me that she experiences me as carrying her in my mind and wants me to put into words my subjective sense of her. From a place within me that was as unpredictable to me as it was to her I said, "You look like a sad little kitten"—a disciplined spontaneous engagement. I might have said, "Well what do you think?" which I was certain would be a further turnoff. Or I might have said simply, "You look so sad." The effect would have been unpredictable but would have conveyed no novelty, no improvisation, and no expression of my individuality. The progress we can track is revealed by the effect of Sonya's willingness to accept my proposal of an antidepressant. But not quite. I might have ignored her holdout: "But I don't want to." Instead, I chose to open an inquiry about it. My mode of inquiry was to offer the information I held in mind about reasons for her reluctance and wonder whether she had anything to add, that is to move us forward. Sonya's response about not liking Dr. N, which I had not known, expanded our exploration. I was confronted again with a choice. Under most circumstances, I would have asked a patient to tell me what she didn't like about Dr. N, almost routinely fitting that inquiry into the flow of the session. Instead I chose to offer an alternative as a direct provision. I made my choice rapidly without considering my usual alternative. The explanation I offered myself after the session was that I was so eager to get Sonya to follow through on the consultation, I spontaneously did what I thought would best persuade her.

Weeks later, I discovered through what seemed like a chance association that we had been involved in an enactment of a significant event in Sonya's adolescence. She had pleaded with her mother not to make her keep going to an orthodontist. Her mother would not listen to Sonya's fear-driven pleading that something was amiss with the dentist. Later newspaper articles documented the charge of a number of girls that he had been sexually abusive. Without conscious knowledge of the role I was enacting, I had reversed the position of her mother's insensitive, uncaring "no" in my immediate acceptance of her desire not to return to Dr. N. Although I had and have every reason to respect Dr. N's integrity, in my immediate acceptance of her desire not to return to him, I gave my authority to her desire.

The pivotal communication in the session, the metaphor of the sad little kitten, had ramifications outside of its descriptive aptness. After Sonya bought her "kitty" and she (the kitten) became a regular subject for us, she revealed that cats had played a role in her family life. Her mother always had a cat. Her brother treated the cat as if it were his and, in typical fashion, was as sadistic to the cat as he had been to Sonya. This gave identificatory meaning to Sonya that she, like the sad little kitten, was her brother's victim, unprotected by her impotent, childish mother. As I reflected on my unexpected choice of metaphor, I was startled to remember that at a time when one of my daughters was going through a troubled spell, she had insisted on having a kitten of her own. We had gotten her an adorable marmalade kitten. Tragically, during a house move, the kitten had run out into the street and been killed. This troubling memory was filled with guilt, remorse, and sadness. My disciplined spontaneous communication condensed Sonya's unhappiness, my daughter's unhappy face, and the runover kitten with the expression of sadness Sonya and I had shared.

Tracking the microprocesses of the session points to a sequence that moved from an unpromising stalemate to an increasingly lively exchange. The stalemate involved both Sonya's obstinate refusal to consider a recommended action and a complete suspension of dialogue between us. The kitten metaphor intervention led to Sonya's becoming open to my proposal that she go for a medication consultation. From the standpoint of the process during the session, the metaphor led to a rapid verbal exchange in which Sonya revealed hitherto unavailable information. By following the sequence, we can recognize several positive effects of the intervention: an improved dialogue, Sonya's shift from obstinate refusal resulting in a dramatic shift in the ambiance between us, and a further series of informative associations and revelations.

Progress can be evaluated on a broader scale by following the sequence beginning in the session itself and observing subsequent actions and later sessions. This wider tracking reveals forward movement in the treatment. Resilience or the capacity to self-right after the removal of an obstacle provides one measure of progress. Our sharing of the affect state symbolized by the poor little kitten was followed by a dramatic self-righting to a higher state of integration and, less dramatically, by my telling her she could go to another neuropharmacologist. What was the obstacle that had been removed? The little kitten intervention helped to counter her absolute conviction that no one appreciated *her* suffering. My offer of a new referral helped to counter her fixed belief that no one listened to her. The still more dramatic rebound that occurred after the change of medication resulted from the removal of a physiological obstacle of brain chemistry.

A second measure of progress lies in a jointly expanding awareness of self with self and self with other. The conventional view of expanding awareness or insight focused only on patients' learning about the nature and origin of their symptoms or personality disturbances. Along with many contemporary relationists and self psychologists, the view I hold expands the conventional view from symptoms and personality disturbances to include patients increasing their awareness of patterns of self with other and of intimacy with self. In instances in which the "other" is the therapist, patients gain insight into whom they are to the therapist and the therapist to them; therapists increase their awareness of the same. But "joint" means something more. Joint refers to a process whereby the subjective expansion of patient and therapist is made possible by their interplay during the clinical exchange while that interplay itself becomes a subject of expanding awareness. Sonya learned that her hopelessness and obstinate refusals were not set in concrete. Happily, she discovered that she could open her stance to negotiation once she felt her mind-state was being fully understood conceptually and especially emotionally. From my reflection on the shared moment, I learned how moved I had been by her plight. I could recognize that I was suspended between a desire to relieve her distress and a deep conviction that movement out of the mire of pathos required being in it with her and not trying to push beyond her willingness to move.

Subsequently the shared moment led us in different but related directions of exploration. Sonya revealed the prior experiences of cats in her life—her mother's preference for them, her brother's desperate dependence and mistreatment of the family cat, and Sonya's identification with the cat's abused and unprotected state. Sonya also revealed the story of being forced to go to the orthodontist. I came to appreciate the special linkage in my mind of Sonya to my daughter and the runover kitten.

My awareness included something additional. I had learned that to establish a relational space with Sonya, I had to forgo the kind of inquiry and exploration (conceptual space) as a joint project that I value highly. Inquiry and exploration was mine alone to carry. Our interplay was more centered on doing—that is, maintaining contact and building a repository of information I could use to understand her. Sonya had little capacity for reflective functioning, and what she had she would use only rarely and never on "request." Thus, I acted—"I'll give you another referral." I connected the cat stories and the orthodontist stories to our spontaneous exchange, but Sonya neither explicitly connected nor explicitly valued such connections when I offered them to her. She did value our joint ownership of stories about her kitten and the kitty's pranks and clearly valued the companionship of the kitten as affectionate and loved housemate.

A significant criterion for change lies in a reorganization of established patterns of relating to one's self and to others. The reordering of representations or maps or schemas of how one is to be in the world involves changes in feelings, priorities, initiatives, values, and attachment strategies. Reordering of self with other schemas provides the greatest likelihood of the persistence of positive changes brought about in therapy despite the stresses of time. Increased resilience or self-righting confers a greater ability to respond to any momentary stress. Yet even a rebound as striking as Sonya's to the intervention of the sad kitten moment plus the antidepressant's physiological lift may do little in itself to bring about more lasting change. Also, for Sonya, an increased awareness of relevant stories of her past may help to create a more coherent narrative, but had limited permanence in the face of Sonya's entrenched strategy of delinking past and present, of seeing herself as a person without memory. Nonetheless, in the sequence I described, one set of representations of self with other did become dislodged and open to reorganization.

To appreciate the significance of the reorganization of symbolic representations made possible in the session, I must first de-dramatize the event. From the beginning of our sessions together, I had demonstrated to Sonya that I would neither be silent nor intrude without a cue to speak. Rather, I would remain as close to her depressed, pessimistic perspective as I could while holding out an alternative optimism. Thus, the session contains nothing new, including the ongoing recommendation for a renewed medication consultation. Yet the stuckness came unstuck. Was it the novelty of the metaphor with its many completely unconscious (to me) linkages to her life and mine? Was it a special quality of feeling, of authenticity and freshness because of my out-of-awareness identifying Sonya with my daughter and the concern, guilt, and compassion that association condensed into my face and voice? Without the prior innumerable moments of connection, it wouldn't have happened, but it was more than one more increment in connection, a more dramatic shaking up and reshaping than that. I believe the total communication inherent in the sad kitten metaphor produced for Sonya a cognitive–affective discrepancy between her conviction that no one would appreciate *her* suffering and devote himself to relieve it and the caring and concern and provision I was offering. It was not a new discrepancy but a new and pivotal appreciation of an ongoing one.

The reorganization went beyond her revising her pessimistic conviction that it was futile to follow my recommendation. That was the immediate impact. The major reorganization followed the lift (unfortunately only temporary) from the antidepressant. Sonya as a small child had been fond of her father (as later associations revealed) until becoming painfully disillusioned after his divorcing her mother and remarrying an unwelcoming stepmother. Sonya was further disillusioned by a failed love affair in graduate school and subsequently refused all dating, becoming cold and abrasive to men, whom she saw only as "hitting on her." I found it easy to regard Sonya as attractive, feminine, and potentially a sensual partner for a man who could appreciate her intelligence and ironic, satirical wit. I believed, however, that she gave me no opening to explore her absolute avoidant turnoff of men. Nothing in the overt transference to me gave any indication that an unconscious reconsideration was taking place. The best view of me I saw Sonya having was that I was a conscientious, reliable, genderless not-mother, not-father, and not-brother. Stated differently, Sonya in her depression was so caught up in early needs for securing an attachment (primarily maternal) that the later desires of an oedipal-age girl for a sensual–erotic linkage to a man were nowhere in evidence. Then suddenly they emerged and continued straight into Sonya's eventual marriage. Sonya's acquiring her kitten, perhaps our joint child—an image Sonya would have protested against vehemently—made another change that was to persist. Sonya's hold on human connections rested on work associates and a network of former female school friends in other cities. She had been lonely and alone. The kitten entered her life as a playful companion, and now Sonya could live out being a provider who, unlike her childhood experience, was not being exploited and abused. Kitty took what was willingly given but gave back an attachment that made Sonya feel wanted and appreciated. An implicit relational knowing (mapped in representations or brain schemas) was now reverberating between Sonya and me and Sonya and kitty.

What are indications of progress in the microprocesses of a session or in several contiguous sessions? An obvious answer is that the discourse becomes more collaborative. That answer is tricky, however, because what might be evaluated as a collaborative effect of a therapist's intervention is context determined. Becoming more succinct is a positive indicator for a patient who has been chattering away in a preoccupied discursive manner. Becoming less succinct is a positive indicator for a patient who has been avoidant, withholding, overly clipped, or obsessional. Becoming freer emotionally is generally a positive indicator for the many patients who are reluctant to express anger, shame, fear, sadness, or joy, sensual arousal, affection, or longing. Becoming less free emotionally, that is, more regulated, is a positive indicator for patients easily prone to affect states of rage, panic, paralyzing shame, guilt, depression or euphoria, passion, or rapture.

After an intervention, we are generally pleased to find that a patient's associations are more coherent and accessible to understanding. Such a response from the patient indicates a sense of being understood and safe. Feeling understood and safe can, however, facilitate a period of creative chaos and disorder in associations and emotions. Creative flux may herald the dissolution of rigidly held beliefs and expectations. The way to an altered vision and freer choices may become open. The reordering may be as noteworthy as Sonya's getting her kitten and beginning to date. Or the reordering may be as subtle as a change of speech patterns. A patient who has routinely avoided responsibility through circumlocutions such as "well one might suppose" or "it could happen that" can signal progress through a linguistic shift from a passive to an active verb and from an indefinite to a personal pronoun: "I insist that. . . ." A patient who had assumed herself responsible for every unhappy event demonstrated progress when she becomes open to recognize the dyadic nature of disruptive interplay with the therapist or with others. Progress after an intervention in a session can be noted when a patient can become more aware of his bodily needs.

This list of indicators of a patient's positive responses to a therapist's communication during a session can be reversed to indicate lack of progress or the hardening of a problematic attitude, belief, or resistant stance.

Sylvia was described in chapter 4, where I tracked the message containing her message about missing people she cared about. The following session deals with her response to her collagen tissue disease and its effect on her sense of self-worth. Tracking the interchange reveals therapist and patient in close collaboration through much of the session until the therapist's heavy-handed interventions goaded her into a loss of the flexible attitude she had achieved and into a hardening of her more rigid all-or-nothing stance.

PATIENT: I'm a little behind—I wanted to get the house done before my sister arrived—but it's not too bad—I got a fair amount done.
THERAPIST: So you feel pretty good about it, even if you didn't get the whole thing finished?

PATIENT: Yeah, but it is hard not to have it completely done because I have a picture in my mind of how I want it to look.
THERAPIST: Tell me about that.

PATIENT: Well, because of my body I can't get everything done I want to get done.
THERAPIST: Is there something you say to yourself about this?

PATIENT: I do it more in terms of limits—once in a while I push myself really hard—like this week—to see what I can do.
THERAPIST: To see what your capacity is?

PATIENT: Yeah, but last night I knew I wasn't going to get the place cleaned and organized the way I wanted to.

THERAPIST: So you looked back at what you'd done and came up with an assessment?

PATIENT: Yeah.
THERAPIST: And what was your feeling about how it went?

PATIENT: That I have more plans than I have energy and strength.
THERAPIST: Uh-huh.

PATIENT: I'm trying to come up with a magic formula.
THERAPIST: And what would a magic formula look like?

PATIENT: How can I optimize it—and I'm getting better at balancing it. Like tonight S (daughter) has a program to go to and my sister is coming in tomorrow, so I decided I need to accept the fact that I wasn't going to get the apartment the way I wanted.
THERAPIST: So it sounds like you are learning that you have to keep some energy in reserve for the things you want to do.

PATIENT: Right, because if I don't, I get really tired.
THERAPIST: Bone tired.

PATIENT: Yeah—because that's hard to recover from—plus I'm learning to cut corners.
THERAPIST: Not to be such a perfectionist about the job you're doing? [The therapist underscores Sylvia's being less of a perfectionist, that is, being more flexible, to make explicit the progress he views Sylvia to be making.]

PATIENT: Yeah, and I'm trying not to give up the things that are important to me.
THERAPIST: So this is not just about testing your strength but also about figuring out how you can find a balance.

PATIENT: Right—and like last night when I pushed it too far—I can learn from that.
THERAPIST: So the next time you can be more cautious.

PATIENT: Right, but it's not the same in every situation—you have to judge based on how you're feeling because sometimes you can do more than other times. But if I learn to know when I'm pushing it too far I can back off before I get overtired.
THERAPIST: Well it sounds like you are learning to read the signals from your body. [Here the therapist is helping Sylvia recognize the reflective awareness that helps her to be flexibly responsive.]

PATIENT: Yeah, that's what I'm trying to do.
THERAPIST: And give those signals some importance.

PATIENT: Right, but I do get less done—but that's OK.
THERAPIST: And you feel like that would be a good trade-off.

PATIENT: Yeah, but I still feel bad that I didn't complete the work.
THERAPIST: But this is tolerable for you?

PATIENT: As long as I stay busy.
THERAPIST: Because if you stay busy, you can't accuse yourself of being lazy?

PATIENT: Well, it's more about comparing myself to other people.
THERAPIST: And how does that go? [The therapist makes an assumption that Sylvia corrects and he follows her.]

PATIENT: Well, they are faster than me. And in the end what matters is how much I got done compared to somebody else. Like the two old women who clean my house in four hours—I'm never going to work that fast—no matter how hard I try. And that's what really matters in the end, and that really bothers me.
THERAPIST: So what do you say to yourself, "I can't even keep up with a couple of old ladies?" [I believe the therapist begins to come across as too heavy-handed, as pressing Sylvia in a way that can be heard as mocking.]

PATIENT: Well, I just can't keep up—even if I took breaks I couldn't get it done in a day—plus if you think about it, it really is pretty depressing.

THERAPIST: So does that have the effect that it diminishes what you can do—what you are able to do?

PATIENT: Yeah—but I'm not so bad when I'm by myself.

THERAPIST: But when you bring another person into the picture, you can't help but compare.

PATIENT: Yeah.

THERAPIST: You know it sounds like you are comparing yourself to this other person—in this case these two cleaning women—but leaving your physical illness out of the equation.

PATIENT: Right—but that's because in the end, it's all about how much you actually get done. [Sylvia does not like to be explicitly confronted about having a debilitating illness, and her attitude begins to harden.]

THERAPIST: But don't you feel like it's a bit unfair to compare yourself to two healthy women who are professional housecleaners and not consider the impact that your illness has on your ability to do this kind of work?

PATIENT: Why, because it's not my fault?

THERAPIST: Well, yeah I guess so—your illness is not something you've chosen for yourself—it doesn't feel like a fair comparison. [From this point on, the discourse degenerates into an argument with Sylvia retreating to her defensive position of viewing herself as a failure and the therapist trying to reason her out of it. The gain in flexibility is, for the moment, lost as an unrecognized enactment replaces the prior collaborative communication.]

PATIENT: Right, but you can compare for effort and I think I win pretty much—which is good—but the end result is still what matters.

THERAPIST: So what happened to the effort calculation?

PATIENT: What do you mean?

THERAPIST: Well, it sounds like by saying that result is still what matters, you are leaving out the effort calculation.

PATIENT: Yeah, I guess so—but what's the matter with that? Anything other than looking at the end result is just an excuse, it doesn't change the fact that I didn't get as much done as someone else.

THERAPIST: So you're not going to accept any excuses—for you the only thing that matters is how much gets done in the end.

Patients having negative responses to a therapist's verbal, gestural, or silent communication are an inevitable consequence of the effort by both participants to bring sensitive areas to the fore. Although as therapists we often seek to facilitate positive responses, we recognize that negative responses frequently result in highly desirable changes. Sometimes the positive effect is the patient's sense of efficacy in being able to object and stand up for herself. At other times the progress comes about as the result of successful exploration of a disruption of the empathic bond between them that results from the aversive response.

In one startling example of a disruption followed by repair and exploration, I attempted to convey my understanding from within the perspective of a patient. I believed I was using Leah's own words when she suddenly erupted with anger, completely disrupting the previous flow. Leah's family was of Eastern European Jewish origin. I tried to say to her that I understood how hard she had tried to remain close to her mother's heart in accord with her mother's wishes. For heart I tried to use her and her mother's Yiddish word. My pronunciation, however, was more the German used by my grandparents. Leah erupted with scathing fury. "Heart. You wouldn't know anything about heart. You're one of the German Jews who looked down on us. Your kind are responsible for the shame my family felt as struggling immigrants." After my startle at her eruption, I took up (wore) her attribution. I acknowledged our difference in background and the humiliation caused by the arrogance of presumed superiority. We went back and forth with this issue in an unusually lively dialogue indicating a restoration of trust and openness to inquiry. I offered my conjecture that her persistent distrust of me and the tension between us that resulted from it might have a source in this ethnic difference. She left this suggestion hanging in the air in a long silence at the end of the session. The next session, she reported a dream of being threatened by a Nazi. We used the disruptive intervention and the dream image–metaphor to bring more fully into awareness her hitherto (to me) puzzling source of distrust of me.

The microprocesses embedded in disruption–restoration sequences are complex and require tracking prior sequences to understand any one experience. In my therapy with Leah, after a difficult opening phase, we had established a rhythm in which most of my attempts to intervene from her perspective were met by her with indicators that she felt understood and could move on. Therefore, the context of this disruptive intervention, a dramatic example of a failed attempt at empathic mirroring, occurred against a background of positive experiences. I think of it as having a reserve of goodwill to draw on at times of need. During a period filled with disagreements as in the early phase of Leah's treatment, every possible negative expectation of this seriously phobic, easily hurt, and offended patient had seemed confirmed by my silent listening or spoken discourse. Were we to have been in such an aversive ambiance, the current disruption would have seemed simply more of the same rather than a discrepant event. Without that disparity, the possibility of a creative flux and a forward-moving restoration would have been far less.

A frequent challenge for a therapist (or a patient) is to recognize that a disruption has occurred. Recognition is easy when a disruption is eruptive, as with Leah, but disruptions can be as subtle as a change in tone or a loss of vitality in the patient's ongoing narrative. Or the disruption may be evidenced by a retreat from a more balanced and nuanced perspective to absolutes and rigidities. Similarly, the therapist's contribution to the disruption is obvious when the patient reacts to a spoken comment with an immediate aversive manifestation such as Leah's antagonism or a patient's withdrawal into silence or even sleep. The therapist's contribution is more difficult to identify when the patient's cohesion and collaboration is affected by the therapist's silence, not the silence of empathic listening, but the silence of failing to pick up on a cue to speak, to indicate involvement and understanding or to return from a moment of being distracted. Other difficult to identify sources that sometimes lead to a disruption may be actions by the therapist that he or she does not even know are silently influencing the patient. Examples are an upcoming time away, an unmentioned reaction to a bill, something the patient heard about the therapist, a chance informal encounter, or even a "sighting" of the therapist outside the office that the therapist doesn't know about.

Therapists contribute to a repair of a disruption linearly and nonlinearly. A linear contribution results from the therapist's spoken words. After some conceptual processing in inner speech, therapists contribute to the explicit recognition of what is happening as they perceive it and open an inquiry into their and the patient's experiencing and understanding of the event. A nonlinear contribution to the repair of a disruption derives from the respect therapists convey to patients through their willingness to wear an attribution and to explore its meaning with an open mind in a spirit of inquiry.

Developmental trauma originates not only from what parents or others do to children but also from the way it is handled afterward. The assault on the child's subjectivity from verbal, physical, or sexual abuse is made far worse by subsequent parental indifference, denial, disavowal, and blaming of the child. When therapists take up the disruptive experience through an authentic willingness to explore their contribution to its triggering, they introduce an unconsciously registered (sometimes consciously recognized) discrepancy between the current experience and past experiences with parents or themselves. Discrepant experiences activate comparator functions in the brain and force change in networks or schemas. I believe therapists responding to disruptions in these ways helps to strengthen and promote resilience and self-righting. Self-righting operates dyadically. As a patient evidences resilience, a therapist gains confidence that an empathic failure or even mildly traumatic occurrence, such as suddenly becoming ill during a session, can be recovered from more readily. This in turn promotes the therapist's own self-righting.

Often all that can be accomplished after a disruption is damage control, that is, the restoration of a prior level of discourse, metaphorically putting the pieces back together more or less as they were. Yet especially as a therapy moves along, we can aim for more. The key to accomplishing more often rests on whether a patient has been able to join the therapist in a spirit of inquiry. When a patient can explicitly or implicitly become curious about what has transpired between himself and his therapist, the exploration of the meaning of the disruption opens to a potentially widening range of associations. Curiosity-inspired exploration employs a linear search for meaning using reasoning and the pool of information provided by the patient and therapist's associations. Of course, the same can be said about any productive therapy moment. The difference lies in the nonlinear sense of urgency a disruption in a functioning dyad stimulates. To understand something that matters to a patient always has exploratory motivation, but to sort out something upsetting that has happened between the patient and the therapist has an extra charge of attachment urgency.

Findings that characterize progress in a session or contiguous sessions and those that characterize more persisting change are not easily distinguished. An increased ability to sense and appraise transactions between oneself and another or others is observable both in the microprocess of a session and as a long-range trend. These valuable capacities have been called metacognition, mentalization, reflective functioning, an opening to "thirdness," and possessing a theory of mind. Traumatized individuals who have a limited capacity for reflective functioning are more prone to borderline disorders than others who have had equal or worse trauma. Progress can then be measured by a patient's growing capacity to be both self-reflective and able to sense into the minds of others. This measure is clinically complex in that it comprises numerous factors. We see progress when patients who have followed an out-of-awareness procedural pattern to treat people arrogantly and sadistically, to be submissive, or to provoke mistreatment can recognize that their thinking, their decision making, enters into their action patterns in any way. Simple recognition can be the precursor for reflection and taking of responsibilities.

Progress in reflection is often not a direct effect of therapy's encouragement of openness to be thoughtful but the indirect result of increased regulation of emotion. During affect states of rage, panic, depression, humiliation or euphoria, or dissociative states of blankness and deadness, patients have cognitive disturbances in functioning that preclude the distancing required for reflection on their state or the contexts that might help to explain it. Another factor that indicates progress in reflection is patients' ability to decenter from their singular point of view and to consider the perspective and feelings of another. At a more developed level, progress for a patient involves not only the recognition of the mind-state of another person but an appreciation of the meaning of the interplay between the patient and that person. Finally, recognition can, one hopes, include the intersubjective field that has been cocreated by the participants in any relationship. Especially in the ending phase of a successful therapy, reverie and lively exchange can move back and forth to reveal deeper levels of reflective possibility.

I have described the value of tracking progress in functional capacities over extended sequences in an exploratory treatment. Self-righting, joint expanding awareness, rearrangement of symbolic schemas, and increased reflective functioning are useful signposts to indicate success. The more conceptual signposts often point to changes that have already occurred in the therapist–patient relationship. In turn, increased awareness and reflection make possible further conceptual, relational, and communicative progress, an unbroken circularity.

I now shift the focus to changes in the relationship. To institute the treatment, patient and therapist must be willing to accept the other based on relatively little knowledge. The degree to which each accepts the other remains a background factor throughout treatment. Sometimes acceptance or rejection moves into the foreground as in a patient's decision to quit or a therapist's decision to refer the patient to someone else. With Sonya, her acceptance of me increased in what seemed to me infinitesimally small increments, mine of her more rapidly. Accepting another only has meaning to the extent that the other can be known. Sonya did not want herself to be known by me (or by herself, as evidenced by her blotting out her memory).

She placed considerable constraint on the extent to which I could be transparent to her.

Through their speech, accent, attire, office, punctuality, billing, facial expression, and body language, therapists continuously disclose aspects of themselves and the manner in which they are approaching their treatment of a particular patient. However much is conveyed in this manner, important aspects of an individual's more essential humanity is left out. Just as a patient's symptoms and history and more formal presentation in the consulting room omit a deeper sense of who he is, so a therapist's style of interviewing, listening, and interpreting fail to reveal much about him that the patient really wants and often needs to know. So the transparency of each participant to the other is an aspect of progress. With Sonya, my freedom to become more open received a big lift as we talked about the kitten's needs to play, to be fed, to sleep, to go to the vet, to get shots, and so on.

A later exchange exemplifies this freedom. Sonya came to her session obviously unwell with a bad upper respiratory infection. She described how terrible she felt and all the work she had to do at her office, probably staying late this evening to get it done. My questioning her need to return to work evoked her usual refusal, and we fell into the familiar stalemated silence of our earlier days. As the session was coming to an end, she looked at me and asked "What?" about my facial expression. I told her I was having a fantasy of picking her up, carrying her to her home, putting her in her bed, taking her temperature, which I thought was elevated, and getting her some warm broth (no chicken soup, knowing she was a vegetarian). She broke a silence with "OK. I'll go home. Kitty must be getting desperate; I've been working so late every night." Increasing transparency of either patient or therapist or of both is not in itself necessarily an indication of progress. What each increasingly reveals to the other must be found to be acceptable to the recipient. This was dramatically played out in the *Sopranos* TV show when Tony revealed not only his seduction of one of his therapist's other patients but his potential to threaten the therapist, a threat that for him could be tantamount to murder.

In the Coda that ends the book, I will consider progress as it evolves from each of the guidelines.

CODA

THERAPISTS HAVE CONCEPTUALIZED PROGRESS in different ways as our understanding of psychopathology and therapy has evolved. Originally insight, described as rendering the unconscious conscious, was emphasized. In this depiction, the goal was to be as exact or explicit as possible about the nature of intrapsychic conflict and its origins in childhood. Progress was measured by the success of a therapist's understanding and verbal articulation and a patient's ability to follow and accept a linear path of explanation. The therapist–patient relationship was a necessary vehicle (a working alliance) to be kept as unintrusive as possible. Pushed by a widening scope of patient selection, the dyadic nature of mutual influence came more to the foreground of explanations of how exploratory treatments were to be achieved. The factors that could be regarded as progress, such as increased relational knowing or a movement from insecure to secure attachment, became more implicit. With this shift from predominantly explicit to both explicit and implicit factors, additional changes in perspective occurred. An emphasis on the negative (conflictual) as the primary source of therapeutic focus shifted to a more balanced view that included attempts to understand and promote positive experience as well. Regulation, especially of affect, and the increased importance given to reflective ability to sense one's own mind-states and that of others introduced more implicit influences.

As the interplay of factors that might be influencing immediate and long-term progress became more complex, predictability and certainty gave way to a nonlinear approach. The nonlinear, inexplicit influences called on therapists to regard context, perspective, and multidimensionality as conceptual frameworks that give to each therapist–patient dyad its own uniqueness. Rules and rituals of therapy give way to spontaneity and improvisation, but only to a degree. Through the principles of technique I have selected, I attempt to balance stability with spontaneity and consistency with creative flux. Evaluating progress means taking into account what is occurring both explicitly and implicitly through linear and nonlinear processes.

Arrangements that establish a frame of friendliness, consistency, reliability, and an ambiance of safety create an explicit structure of meeting times, place, fees, frequency, and mutual obligations. The framework of consistency allows for creative variability in occasional ad hoc switching of session times or the use of phone sessions during absences or times of emergent need. A growing ambiance of security indicates progress, sometimes in the foreground as an explicitly experienced affect of safety, and more often in the background as an implicit basis for either or both patient and therapist to feel freer to be more open and direct in their verbal and nonverbal communication.

Progress in the systematic application of the empathic mode of perception is the linchpin of therapeutic success because so many implicit and explicit consequences result from it. As therapists increase their ability to view experience from the point of view of their patients, they build up a memory bank of the patients' past and present. They carry the schema of their patients in their minds and draw on it to understand and respond more effectively to communications in each session. Implicitly this allows therapists to make subtle adjustments in their phrasing, tone of voice, gesture, and emphasis. Explicitly they can offer patients the view they hold of them for affirmation or revision. For patients, explicit gains include (1) the sense that they are understood when they are, (2) being able to revise a view that is faulty, and (3) being able to have an impact on the therapist. An implicit gain for patients is that increased awareness of their state of mind enhances their capacity to be self-reflective and to be reflective about the state of mind of others, including their therapist.

As therapists become more skilled in sensing into their patients' state of mind, they recognize more about the patients' emotions and mode of thinking, the status of their patients' initiative, and their patients' view of themselves and others (especially the therapist). This view of empathic perception as including cognition, representational maps, motivation, and emotion constitutes an integrated whole with shifts in what therapists can recognize to be most salient at any time in the foreground. Within this framework of shifting emphasis, our third principle concentrates attention on affects in two ways. We can appreciate progress first as we and our patients are increasingly able to recognize the emotions they actually experience in an event under consideration and second as we and they can discern the emotion they were seeking. Recognizing and discussing an affect being experienced has a regulatory effect; distressing, intense activating affects such as rage, fear, and psychic pain can be diminished and soothed. Distressingly intense dampening affects such as depression, shame, humiliation, and guilt can be helped to be less deadening and more vital as hope is restored through shared understanding.

As therapist and patient succeed in distinguishing an affect experienced during an event from an affect sought (assuming they are different), the patient is helped to repair a common conceptual hangover from childhood thinking—namely, that an outcome is equivalent to an intention. Patients' (or therapists') use of this teleological reasoning is usually entirely out of their awareness. If the pursuit of a patient's striving unfortunately ends in harm to others or to the self, the patient's automatic assumption that he intended to harm others (domination or sadism) or himself (submission or masochism) leads to much unwarranted assessing of blame, shame, and guilt. Important progress in therapy occurs when instances of misapplied assessment of blame can be separated from those instances in which the conscious or unconscious intent is to seek momentary or long-term power over others through reactive or eruptive acts of aggression or by activating the involvement of others through submission and withdrawal.

Most patients begin therapy with a limited awareness of how rich in explicit and especially implicit meaning their communications are. As therapists come to appreciate the various ways in which the "message contains the message," they help patients to increase their sensitivity to the explicit information they convey verbally and gesturally. In the byplay of discourse about the message as communicated, patients learn the subtleties and nuances of the manner in which they experience their moment-to-moment world. As communication is progressively opened to its fullest revelation, patients and therapists pick up the metaphors, ambiguities, and double entendres embedded in speech, facial expression, bodily movements, and gestures. Unexpected linkages become suddenly available, leading to moments of unexpected expanding insight.

Filling the narrative envelope gives the message contained in the message the breath, scope, and liveliness needed for therapists to appreciate empathically their patients' perspective. Initially, therapists move the treatment forward by helping patients to recognize the part of the "story" they have omitted and perhaps the basis for the deletion. As patients become better tellers of the story of their experience, they become better observers. Moreover, a fuller story enables more open reflection about the meaning and impact of the event. An implicit by-product of a more explicit narrative of a biographic self is an increased sense of continuity, cohesion, and unity that patients commonly come to feel at the finish of successful intensive psychotherapy.

Communications become more alive through filling the narrative envelope and expanding revelations from the communicative discourse through recognition that each message contains in it a rich potential for sharing information. These are ongoing processes throughout therapy. In contrast, wearing a patient's attributions contributes dramatic moments to therapeutic progress. These are moments when patient and therapist open themselves to both greater risk and greater potential for immediate progress. The patient risks an unpleasant encounter with the therapist as she explicitly or implicitly reveals to the therapist whom he has become for her. If the attribution is unflattering, critical, and hostile, the patient risks a backlash. If the attribution is overly idealized or expresses extreme dependence, as in "You are the most important person in my life, I can't live without you," the patient risks a painful disclaimer and rebuff. A therapist allowing himself to wear an attribution risks a painful recognition about himself, the loss of a comfortable idealized position, or both. The potential gain in progress, however, warrants the risk for both parties. Wearing the attribution and opening the discourse to discovering who patient and therapist have come to be for each other opens the way to a nonlinear reordering of the symbolic representation of each to the other and to the self.

The discourse that takes place as therapist and patient struggle to depict and understand an attribution presents a patient with three explicit representational schemas with which to conjure. In the immediate foreground is the representation of the therapist conveyed in the specific attribution with its implicit link to a past (transference) self-with-other experience. The obvious or subtle cue emanating from the therapist that triggered the attribution belongs to this representation. Second is a remembered representation of the more usual way the patient has experienced the therapist, sometimes very different from the attribution or, if similar, at least less intense. Third is the therapist in the here and now dialoguing open-mindedly with the patient as they play with each view of the attribution. As he listens, seeks the source of the attribution, and remains open to play with the dyadic nature of the images and issues despite the discomforts that they may evoke in him, he in effect offers the patient a newly discrepant, but therapeutically potent, image of himself.

To recapitulate, more or less simultaneously, three discrepant views of the therapist coexist: the view in the attribution, the remembered usual view, and the immediate view of the therapist open-mindedly participating in the exploration of the attribution. What gives these divergent experiences of the therapist by the patient its transformational potential? A patient's making an attribution and having a therapist "wear" it creates a dramatic moment that disrupts the more routine flow of the therapy. The flux and play that ensues opens the path to change and the reopening of reflective space. My experience has been that positive transformations already in progress accelerate after incidents of dyadic negotiation spurred by joint exploration of attributions. How these transformations occur is a matter of speculation. My hypothesis is based on the brain functioning of comparator detectors that are sensitive to disparities. When a small disparity in an expectation occurs, the comparator institutes a revision in an existing category, such as a self-with-other schema or map. When an intense traumatic discrepancy of an expectation occurs, the comparator detector may be unable to cope with the affective storm without resorting to dissociation or other major defensive means. When a moderate disparity in an expectation occurs, however, as with the three different representations of the therapist in the byplay of wearing an attribution, a more extensive reordering of representational maps is able to evolve.

Much of what I describe about the progress that results from therapist and patient working together to explore an attribution applies as well to the dyadic cocreation of model scenes. Working with a model scene is like playing a game in conceptual space. One or the other, usually the patient, tells a story, often a memory, dream, or plot from a movie or book, and the other, usually the therapist, recognizes the explanatory significance of the theme. An immediate sense for both is how the scene reveals a clear metaphoric model of experiences that they had been seeking to lift from the shadows. As with a skeletal outline of a plot, the scene becomes open to embellishments, changes in nuance, and, more important for progress, linking to prior puzzling enactments, symptoms, and rigidly held beliefs. Especially meaningful as an indicator of progress is the patient's and therapist's appreciation that together they have created and shared a small universe of meaning that, like money placed in a joint account, either or both can draw on when needed.

The aversive motivational system requires special attention, but not in the traditional manner. Traditionally, progress was measured by privileging the interpretation of defenses to get behind them and gain access to an unconscious impulse, fantasy, or moral stricture. While each motivational system receives our empathic attention when its manifestations are believed to be in the foreground, the aversive motivational system, when thought to occupy the foreground, is particularly important, because dysregulation of antagonism or withdrawal is crucial to most emotional problems. Evaluating progress in the patient's, the therapist's, and the dyad's approach to aversiveness requires a revised understanding of the workings of what has been called defenses, resistance, or reluctance.

Openness is the key to evaluating progress. But openness to what? Patients become more open to awareness of their anger, fear, sadness, shame, humiliation, embarrassment, and guilt. Patients become alert to what triggers their negative emotions and the patterns of their expression. Therapists also become more open to their own aversive affects, triggers, and modes of expression. Such openness enlarges the realm and forms of self-communication, but it accomplishes still more. At any moment when the aversive (or any other) motivation system appears to be dominant, not only self-regulation but also mutual regulation is occurring. Awareness of aversiveness may be enhanced for the patient, the therapist, and both. Especially important is recognition of changes in the quality and intensity of aversiveness occurring in the interpersonal field. Reflective consideration of the growing awareness adds greatly to explicit progress in regulating aversive manifestations. Progress is not limited to explicit awareness because much subtle aversiveness takes place in the form of implicit enactive communication of manipulation, seduction, depreciation, dissociation, and avoidance. Progress in the implicit enactive realm may occur out of awareness through slow, seemingly imperceptible gains in a sense of safety, collaboration, and in the mutual acceptance of a spirit of inquiry.

Much of what I have described already applies to the progress therapists make by having the timing, phrasing, and affective expression of their interventions become sensitive to the needs of their patients. As the partners in the therapeutic dyad adapt to each other's communications, progress will follow the confidence therapists develop in their understanding of the message and in their becoming relaxed in their interventions. To speak of a therapist's relaxation in the conduct of a therapy fraught with intensive interchanges may seem strange. Nonetheless, as treatment progresses, therapists can experience increased ease based on a growing conviction that the partners in the dyad can react to each other and each survive, and the treatment will survive as well. With this odd type of relaxation, therapists will feel free to bring themselves more on the stage and be intuitively open to humor, metaphor, and disciplined spontaneous engagement.

Three different but interrelated realms are indicative of progress in the dyad that enhances therapists' skill at interventions. Increasing sensitivity to conversational space improves collaboration in the dialogue. Increasing sensitivity to relational space helps to adjust the moving toward without intrusion and the moving away without abandonment. Increasing sensitivity to conceptual space opens the mind play to better appreciate current metaphoric meanings and the creation of new possibilities of meaning. In theory, we can describe a therapist's contribution to conversational, relational, and conceptual metaphoric space that increasingly improve his interventions, but such a description would be arbitrarily one-sided. Conversational, relational, and conceptual spaces only come about as cocreations that wax and wane throughout the therapy.

Finally, what can we say about the increasing ability gained in evaluating progress? What would indicate to therapists that they are better able to track the consequences of their interventions? A problem that always confronts evaluating the response to an intervention lies in the camouflaging of nonacceptance in the form of compliance—the "yes" being spoken and the "but" kept hidden. As the partners increase their knowledge of each other, compliance can be better distinguished from an authentic "yes"; the "but" can be stated overtly and the objection can be a valuable contribution. The main means, however, to evaluate progress being made from tracking responses to an intervention lies in the therapist's increasing skill in predicting the impact of an intervention *before* it is made. The progress I am referring to is largely out of awareness, intuitive, and implicit. It is comparable to a mother learning from observing her baby's responses how and when she will elicit a smile or what rhythm of offering a spoonful of food will be responded to with a well-timed open mouth. It is equally comparable to a father knowing how fast and far his toddler likes the swing to go or how much edge he needs in his tone of voice to get through with a request or command to stop playing and come to dinner without making the child cry or balk. Progress in therapy combines therapists being guided by their intuitively sensing the likely positive impact of an intervention and being free on occasion to risk an intervention outside the known safety zone. Each therapist–patient dyad is unique. Thus, the art of conducting a successful exploratory psychotherapy lies in listening, understanding, and articulating within the boundaries of a predictable intersubjective field of safety while remaining open to humor, novelty, and improvisation.

FINAL THOUGHTS

Throughout this guide to the exploratory psychotherapies, I have focused on the clinical work itself. By using and elaborating numerous conceptualizations of the communications and interactions of therapists and patients, I have attested to the complexity involved in the task of bringing about positive change in troubling emotional conditions. An exploratory therapy has a formal aspect, a "frame," combined with an unpredictable emergence of modes of being together that grow out of the particularities of the dyad. I have described the application of the guides and the principles of technique on which they are based as the craft of therapy, its artistry. I have illustrated the craft in my presentations of many clinical exchanges involving two people engaged in affectively rich explicit and implicit communications. Each dyad struggles more or less successfully with patterns having great persistence interspersed with unexpected episodes of revelation and spontaneity, often after long periods of uncertainty. Where I could, I tried to make clear to the reader the reasoning, logic, and linear aspects of the guidelines and the way they inform the clinical work. Also where I could, I tried to make clear the unpredictable nonlinear aspect of much that emerges when two people immerse themselves in the tensions of troubled and traumatic lived experiences.

A spirit of inquiry is more difficult to make explicit because it refers to an implicit, procedural, nonverbal form of background relatedness comparable to the "curiosity" of a mother and infant learning about each other across the spectrum of all their activities. A spirit by definition is ineffable, a state of mind that affects what occurs during a treatment including, but not restricted to, the activity of exploring. For well-trained therapists who have examined their own lived experience, a spirit of inquiry emerges as part of their being. My hope is that the reader has been able to sense how the spirit of inquiry has animated the clinical narratives I have described.

NOTES

I CHOSE TO WRITE THIS GUIDE IN A RELATIVELY free conversational style rather than with the careful referencing of scientific papers and books. Theories derived from many sources are incorporated into proposals without notation of their origins. I hope to achieve the advantage of having the reader flow along more easily without being frequently interrupted by citations. The disadvantage is that I am unable to credit the many authors whose ideas and approaches I draw on.

The clinical examples I present are previously unpublished or drawn from my prior writings:

The Talking Cure (1983). Hillsdale, NJ: The Analytic Press.
Psychoanalysis and Infant Research (1983). Hillsdale, NJ: The Analytic Press.
Psychoanalysis and Motivation (1989). Hillsdale, NJ: The Analytic Press.
Self and Motivational Systems (1992) with F. Lachmann and J. Fosshage. Hillsdale, NJ: The Analytic Press.
The Clinical Exchange (1996) with F. Lachmann and J. Fosshage. Hillsdale, NJ: The Analytic Press.
Hatred and its rewards: A case illustration. *Psychoanalytic Inquiry*, 20:389–408(2000).

A Spirit of Inquiry (2002) with F. Lachmann and J. Fosshage. Hillsdale, NJ: The Analytic Press.

For more personal references:

Forty-five years of psychoanalytic experiences on, behind, and without the couch. *Psychoanalytic Inquiry*, 15:280–293 (1995).

Experience as a guide to psychoanalytic theory and practice. *Journal of the American Psychoanalytic Association*, 46:17–35 (1998).

I also refer the reader to other major sources for my conceptions and for ideas I discuss. For my references to Freud:

Leonardo da Vinci and a memory from his childhood (1910). *Standard Edition*, 11:59–137. London: Hogarth Press, 1957.

Psychoanalytical notes on an autobiographical account of a case of paranoia (1911). *Standard Edition*, 12:9–82. London: Hogarth Press, 1958.

Introductory lectures on psychoanalysis (1916/1917). *Standard Edition*, 15/16. London: Hogarth Press, 1963.

New introductory lectures on psychoanalysis (1933). *Standard Edition*, 22:5–182. London: Hogarth Press, 1964.

Ellman, S. (1991), *Freud's Technique Papers*. Northvale, NJ: Aronson.

Lichtenberg, J. (1994), How libido theory shaped technique (1911–1915). *Journal of the American Psychoanalytic Association*, 42:727–739.

The reader can gain a background in self psychology from the books by Heinz Kohut and the easy to read commentary by Ernest Wolf. For an understanding of empathy, I recommend three seminal papers and the comprehensive coverage in *Empathy 1* and *2:*

Kohut, H. (1971), *The Analysis of the Self*. New York: International Universities Press.

——— (1977), *The Restoration of the Self*. New York: International Universities Press.

——— (1984), *How Does Analysis Cure?* ed. A. Goldberg and P. Stepansky. Chicago: University of Chicago Press.

Schwaber, E. (1981), Empathy: A mode of analytic listening. *Psychoanalytic Inquiry*, 1:357–392.

Lichtenberg, J. (1981), The empathic mode of perception and alternative vantage points for psychoanalytic work. *Psychoanalytic Inquiry*, 1:329–356.

Ornstein, P. and Ornstein, A. (1985), Clinical understanding and explaining: The empathic advantage point. In: *Progress in Self Psychology, Volume 1*, ed. A. Goldberg. Hillsdale, NJ: The Analytic Press, pp. 43–61.

Wolf, E. (1988), *Treating the Self.* New York: Guilford.

Empathy, Volumes 1 and 2 (1984), ed. J. Lichtenberg, M. Bornstein, and D. Silver. Hillsdale, NJ: The Analytic Press.

Greenson, R. (1967), *The Technique and Practice of Psychoanalysis.* New York: International Universities Press.

Throughout the guide, I utilize findings and concepts of attachment research. Since John Bowlby's initial writings, the literature on attachment research and theory has become voluminous. The reader can find an extensive summary and a contemporary perspective in three issues of *Psychoanalytic Inquiry* edited by Diana Diamond and Sydney Blatt:

Bowlby, J. (1969, 1973, 1980), *Attachment, Separation, and Loss.* New York: Basic Books.

Attachment Research and Psychoanalysis: Theoretical Considerations. *Psychoanalytic Inquiry*, 19:4.

Attachment Research and Psychoanalysis: Clinical Considerations. *Psychoanalytic Inquiry*, 19:5.

Attachment Research and Psychoanalysis: Further Reflections on Theory and Clinical Experience. *Psychoanalytic Inquiry*, 23:1.

Other contributions to the extensive literature on infancy have illuminated my understanding of development:

Stern, D. N. (1985), *The Interpersonal World of the Infant.* New York: Basic Books.

——— (1990), *Diary of a Baby.* New York: Basic Books.

Beebe, B. and Lachmann, F. (2002), *Infant Research and Adult Treatment.* Hillsdale, NJ: The Analytic Press.

Meares, R. (1993), *The Metaphor of Play.* Northvale, NJ: Aronson.

Fivaz-Depeursinge, E. and Corboz-Warnevy, A. (1999), *The Primary Triangle.* New York: Basic Behavioral Science.

Fonagy, P., Gergely, G., Jurist, E., and Target, M. (2002), *Affect Regulation, Mentalization, and the Development of the Self.* New York: Other Press.

Organizing my thinking through a perspective of psychological *systems* derives from Arnold Sameroff and from Esther Thelan and Linda Smith, and in a contemporary version can be found in an issue of *Psychoanalytic Inquiry* edited by Estelle Shane and William Coburn:

Sameroff, A. (1983), Developmental systems: Context and evolution. In: *Mussen's Handbook of Child Psychology, Volume 1*, ed. W. Kessen. New York: Wiley.

Thelen, E. and Smith, L. (1984), *A Dynamic Systems Approach to the Development of Cognition and Action*. Cambridge, MA: MIT Press.

Contemporary Dynamic Systems Theories. *Psychoanalytic Inquiry*, 22:5.

The writings of George Edelman, Antonio Damasio, Allan Schore, and Fred Levin provide a rich background to the neurophysiological systems I employ:

Edelman, G. (1987), *Neural Darwinism*. New York: Harper & Row.

——— (1992), *Bright Air, Brilliant Fire*. New York: Basic Books.

Damasio, A. (1999), *The Feeling of What Happens*. New York: Harcourt Brace Jovanovich.

Schore, A. (1994), *Affect Regulation and the Origin of the Self*. Hillsdale, NJ: Lawrence Erlbaum Associates.

Levin, F. (1991), *Mapping the Mind*. Hillsdale, NJ: The Analytic Press.

I am indebted to Stephen Mitchell, Lewis Aron, Donnel Stern, and Darlene Ehrenberg for their writings on the application of the relational perspective and Jessica Benjamin and Adrienne Harris for their contemporary understanding of the complexity of sexuality and gender:

Mitchell, S. (1993), *Hope and Dread in Psychoanalysis*. New York: Basic Books.

Aron, L. (1999), *A Meeting of Minds*. Hillsdale, NJ: The Analytic Press.

Stern, D. (1997), *Unformulated Experience*. Hillsdale, NJ: The Analytic Press.

Ehrenberg, D. (1992), *The Intimate Edge*. New York: Norton.

Benjamin, J. (1988), *The Bonds of Love*. New York: Pantheon Press.

Harris, A. (1998), Gender as a soft assembly: Tomboys' stories. *Studies in Gender and Sexuality*, 1:223–250.

Much of what I have learned from the colleagues with whom I am in most intimate contact derives not from texts but from often spirited conversation and challenging questioning. While I can't share with the reader these conversations, I can recommend some of their highly informative texts:

Lachmann, F. (2001), *Transforming Aggression*. Northvale, NJ: Aronson.
Fosshage, J. (1983), The psychological function of dreams: A revised approach. In: *Dream Interpretation: A Comparative Study*, ed. J. Fosshage and C. Loew. Cosa Mesa, CA: PMA, pp. 299–318.
Shane, M., Shane, E., and Gales, M. (1997), *Intimate Attachments*. New York: Guilford Press.
Stolorow, R., Brandchaft, B., and Atwood, G. (1987), *Psychoanalytic Treatment: An Intersubjective Approach*. Hillsdale, NJ: The Analytic Press.
Orange, D. (1995), *Emotional Understanding*. New York: Guilford Press.
Slavin, M. and Kriegman, D. (1998), Why the analyst needs to change: Toward a theory of conflict, negotiation, and mutual influence in the therapeutic process. *Psychoanalytic Dialogues*, 8:247–284.
Lichtenberg, J. and Kindler, A. (1994), A motivational systems approach to the clinical experience. *Journal of the American Psychoanalytic Association*, 42:405–420.

While the value of learning from texts and colleagues is undeniable, a therapist's craft and spirit emerges from direct encounters with human emotions and motivations. For myself, I cite the challenges of being a husband, father, and grandfather as well as the experience and opportunity of treating patients and supervising and teaching others. I further cite the continuous challenges of trying to understand my own emotions and motives, and of placing my successes and especially my failures in a context "more human than otherwise" (to paraphrase Sullivan). I believe the reader will appreciate that I feel firmly convinced that the guidelines I propose are clinically valuable. Yet, I also recognize the probable transience of specific recommendations that I and others make. Therapists have been honing their skills and improving their craft since Breuer and Freud with a big boost from Kohut's appreciation of empathy. Beyond the techniques lies the spirit of inquiry and caring. I hope my readers, my patients, and my supervisees take away from my writings and direct encounters an emergent and lasting spirit of inquiry that facilitates their continuing openness to intimacy with their selves and others.

INDEX